Conversations at the Kitchen Table

… Lavish Lunches
and a
Side Dish of Hope

Julie Raguse and Arlene Reindel

xulon
PRESS

Conversations at the Kitchen Table
by Julie Raguse and Arlene Reindel

Printed in the United States of America

ISBN 1-60034-217-5

www.xulonpress.com

Dear Louise,

Please put on a pot of tea or coffee and invite friends and neighbors over for a "conversation at the kitchen table."

Julie Ragure
Arlene Reindel

Acknowledgements...

Thanks to God our Father who caused our paths to cross once again inspiring us to share His lavish, extravagant love with others in these pages. So many people were instrumental in helping us to bring this book to fruition.

Julie…thanks to my husband Marvin and our three sons Karl, Kurt and Ross, my daughter-in-law Ann, and my sister Jean Conklin for their unfailing love and support, especially throughout my life-threatening illness and the writing of this book. Thanks also to my friends Deb Rogner, Joan Ham and Carole Schneider for their continued support, and especially my long-time friend Vicki Charboneau for her encouragement along life's journey.

Arlene – thanks to my sister, friend and prayer partner Denise Werth and her family who are my taste-testers, champions and cheerleaders… and my life-long friends Carol Anderson, Pat Levy, Cheri Skomra, Louise DeKoninck, Nancy Libby, Karen Vaclavik, JoAnn Enekes, Ruth Bouldes, Elizabeth Moore and my three Mikes (you know who you are!) whose abiding love and friendship have blessed me over a lifetime.

Thanks also to Jeannie Morris for hosting a lavish lunch while offering valuable suggestions that greatly improved this book, to Dr. Jim Boldt and his wife Janet who treated us to a lavish brunch and provided guidance on spiritual doctrine, to Vicki Gilbert for her formidable editing skills and to Gloria Pruett, a friend, a mentor and a dramatic testimony to the transforming power of God's handiwork in the life of one who simply trusts Him.

Table of Contents

Introduction

We met in college and crossed paths again 30 years later, discovering a mutual passion for Christ, home-cooked meals and writing. This book contains some of our favorite recipes served up at our kitchen tables, where we shared Scriptural principles and insights that became the cornerstone of our lives and the basis for this book.

Conversations at the Kitchen Table is a collection of 37 faith messages on Christian life followed by discussion questions and lavish lunch recipes. Personal reflections on the hidden treasures in Scripture are paired with easy, nutritious menu suggestions. We hope this will inspire you to gather some friends and neighbors around your kitchen table to share some new recipes and God's abundant love. Our messages are designed to acquaint those who might never pick up a Bible with the timeless message of hope and salvation offered through Jesus Christ.

This book speaks to any age or phase of life. It's for the young who are filled with dreams and trying to bring them to reality. It's for those in mid-life wondering how to juggle too many responsibilities. It's also for those past the prime years, feeling wistful and sad that the best times are in the rearview mirror. We penned these pages to instill hope, faith and a renewed sense of purpose and love for God, who delights in showing himself strong on behalf of those who love Him.

We often marvel at how our friendship languished for decades after college as we pursued lifestyles that couldn't have been more opposite. Yet God was laying down a path that would ultimately reconnect us with an even stronger friendship based on our new identity in Him. This kinship is grounded in His love and a desire to share that with old friends and newcomers alike. The yearning for an everlasting love is satisfied nowhere else but in our Heavenly Father. Once that becomes a reality, it's impossible not to be passionate about sharing it!

Our kitchen tables now serve a dual purpose and so can yours! Besides its everyday use as a place to prepare and serve food, it's a platform for sharing faith. There are people in your sphere of influence, your circle of family, friends, neighbors, and co-workers that no one else can ever reach for God in the way that you can. Use these faith messages, these helpful study/discussion questions, and these wonderful recipes to get started! Gather a group of people who will be blessed to sit at your kitchen table to enjoy food, fellowship and a chance to become acquainted with the one, true God!

A Note from the Authors

Thirty years had passed, but we recognized each other right away when we walked into the café for our reunion lunch in the fall of 2003. We hadn't been seated long and it was like 30 years had vanished in the hours we spent catching up on those missing decades.

We were delighted to discover each had become a Christian over the years. That day was the beginning of a series of lunches where we began to share and write about faith lessons and principles that have enabled us to keep standing in the face of pain, heartache, and the trials of life. This book grew out of those meetings at our kitchen tables. These faith lessons are ones we've lived by....

Arlene...shortly before our reunion lunch, I had recently returned to Michigan from California after taking early retirement. In the last two years, I lost my dad, was diagnosed with breast cancer, and had surgery and follow-up treatment. I decided to return home to spend more time with my widowed mother. I lost her three months later to a stroke. I have no husband, no children and find myself starting over.

Julie...at this writing, I've just been diagnosed with an inoperable tumor in my nasal passage. I'm undergoing an intensive chemotherapy and radiation regimen over the next six months. My husband, three sons, extended family and friends are a great source of strength. My hope is in the Lord who has promised never to leave me or forsake me. I'm trusting in His provision as I undergo this trial.

We hope this collection of essays will be an encouragement to you no matter your age or station in life. This book is addressed to those who are young and just starting out, or more seasoned and discouraged that life has not measured up to those early dreams. It's also for those who feel blissfully content and may be in need of a new Everest to climb. We encourage you to seek out the Lord of the Harvest. *"The harvest is plentiful but the workers are few. Ask the Lord of the harvest, therefore, to send out workers into his harvest field" (Matthew 9:37, 38).*

Wherever you are on this spectrum, let these recipes strengthen your body at the same time these faith messages speak hope to your spirit. This book can be enjoyed individually or utilized as a Bible study with friends and neighbors who want to learn more about the Christian faith and the true God of the Bible. Each message stands on its own and is followed by a series of questions that can prompt a "conversation at the kitchen table." These gatherings centered on Scripture will lead to a deeper understanding of God, how to live according to His purpose, as well as ways to serve Him. The recipes offer lavish lunch suggestions that will please your guests, who are sure to come away enriched in body and soul. Remember that *"man does not live on bread alone, but on every word that comes from the mouth of the Lord" (Deuteronomy 8:3).*

Yours in Christ,

Julie and Arlene
kitchentableministries.com

1

Some Assembly Required...Review Owner's Manual
Check out your Bible...comes with a lifetime warranty!

W e hate reading owner's manuals. We far prefer to trust our intellect, training, instinct and experience and never open a book to get directions or figure out how a thing works. So we career through life spending far too much of it in the dark, in the weeds, in the cross hairs. But what if someone left us an instruction manual that not only revealed the path to eternal life, but how to love, acquire peace, avoid snares and pitfalls, and negotiate the rocky terrain of life? Actually someone did. Our Heavenly Father gave us all this and more in the Bible.

Someone came up with an acrostic for the word "Bible:" *b*asic *i*nstructions *b*efore *l*eaving *e*arth. The Bible is exactly that and more... it's a map, a treasure trove of truth and wisdom, an indispensable tool for the journey, a *"pearl of great price" (Matthew 13:46 KJV)*. Yet the vast majority of Christians leave it on a shelf collecting dust. We hear a sermon from the Bible at church once a week and think that's sufficient.

And it is sufficient if we really don't plan to serve God with all our hearts. It's sufficient if we're unconcerned that our adversary is waiting to strike and that our tools in the natural world are pitiful and ineffective against him. It's sufficient if we don't mind that we'll find ourselves in the same sin battles again and again. It's sufficient if we don't care that our peace will be constantly disturbed, or that we'll be easily discouraged and have little to impart to those who are desperate to hear an uplifting word.

Gosh, sounds like there's some work involved here! Well, okay, let's be honest. By now we all know nothing of value is ever achieved without effort! Serious athletes maintain a regular training regimen whether or not they're facing a competition. We understand the importance of this when it comes to the care of our physical bodies. Yet we totally neglect our spiritual houses that are of far greater importance.

Henry David Thoreau put it this way: "As a single footstep will not make a path on the earth, so a single thought will not make a pathway in the mind. To make a deep physical path, we walk again and again. To make a deep mental path, we must think over and over the kind of thoughts we wish to dominate our lives."

We're not Christians for long before we realize that the thoughts and attitudes of the world are totally opposite to the ways of God. Keeping to the straight path doesn't happen by accident. It means not only relearning and embracing a whole new set of values and beliefs, but rehearsing them on a daily basis. Otherwise, we'll soon find ourselves once more realigned to the world's viewpoint. *"Do not conform any longer to the pattern of this world, but be transformed by the renewing of your mind" (Romans 12:2).*

Swimming upstream and against the tide requires considerable focus and energy. The journey can be lonely, difficult and downright impossible unless we're fortified with God's Word, His blessings and promises. He will help us to keep climbing when the path becomes steep and the terrain more rugged.

Exposing ourselves to Scriptural truth on a daily basis helps it to lodge in our hearts as it lays down new grooves in our minds. Old thoughts and mental constructs die slowly and try to reassert themselves into our consciousness. Battling back with force and clarity is required. *"We demolish arguments and every pretension that sets itself up against the knowledge of God, and we take captive every thought to make it obedient to Christ" (2 Corinthians 10:5).*

If you are a Christian, we hope this book will help you to discover a greater love and a more intimate relationship with God. Coming to Christ is not the end of the journey. It's just the beginning. We were created to bear fruit, and it's only by abiding in Christ that we are able to do so. *"Remain in me, and I will remain in you. No branch can bear fruit by itself; it must remain in the vine. Neither can you bear fruit unless you remain in me. I am the vine, you are the branches…apart from me you can do nothing" (John 15:4-5).*

What's the best way to maintain that branch-to-vine connection? Check your owner's manual on a regular basis!

If you are not a Christian, the joyful message of the Gospel is that the Son of God, Christ our Lord, paid for all of our sins on the cross at Calvary. Through Him alone we are reconnected to the grace of God, having received forgiveness through faith in Christ's atoning work. His shed blood frees us from the punishments of sin and secures our eternity in heaven. We do nothing to earn this awesome act of grace except believe it and receive it. It is a free gift from God our Father and His Son Jesus… the final Passover Lamb.

> *"For God so loved the world that he gave his one and only Son, that whoever believes in him shall not perish but have eternal life" (John 3:16).*

> *"I am the way and the truth and the life. No one comes to the Father except through me" (John 14:6).*

Conversations at the Kitchen Table

- When is the last time you checked your "owner's manual?"

- Is there someone or several "someones" who could do this with you? Can one of these someones become your accountability partner? This is a person with whom you share your weaknesses and vulnerabilities, who prays for and with you and helps to keep you on track in your Christian walk. You do the same for that person.

- Believing the Bible is God's truth is essential for placing our faith and trust in it. What does each of these verses say about Scripture?

  Psalm 119:89
  Matthew 22:29
  John 10:35
  2 Timothy 3:16
  2 Peter 1:20

- *Romans 12:2* says "*...be transformed by the renewing of your mind.*" Can you identify ways in which you are conforming to God's word rather than the world's view?

- Read the Apostle Paul's message to the early church in Corinth in *1 Corinthians 3:2, 3*. Paul gives a milk and solid food analogy for those who lack spiritual wisdom compared to those who are mature in the faith.

  What worldly behavior does Paul see as evidence that the Corinthian church is immature?

  What helps us to mature in our Christian walk?

  What are some things we can do to deepen our faith and not fall back when our lives go dark?

- The Book of Galatians is a powerful, persuasive reinforcement of essential New Testament truths. There are six chapters and it would be a great homework exercise for you and your friends to read a chapter each day this week. Come to the next gathering prepared to discuss what each person felt was the most significant point in each chapter.

Lavish "Book and Author" Lunch

Sitting down with the Bible and getting to know the Author provides direction, imparts wisdom and far surpasses any book and author luncheon we've ever attended! We love soup and this one's a snap to make with whatever vegetables you have in the fridge. Try pairing several together…cauliflower-carrots, broccoli-potato, etc.

Cream of Any Vegetable Soup
3 tablespoons butter
1 small onion, diced
2 tablespoons flour
1 pound any vegetable: asparagus, broccoli, cauliflower, potatoes, spinach, carrots -- rinsed and chopped
4 cups organic chicken or vegetable stock
2 tablespoons fresh, chopped parsley
1 teaspoon salt
Dash pepper
1 teaspoon dried tarragon
1 cup heavy cream or half and half

Rinse and chop veggies of your choice, steam or par-boil 6-8 minutes and place in soup kettle. Add onions and 2 tablespoons butter and cook several minutes until onions are tender. Add the remaining tablespoon of butter and the flour, stirring occasionally until mixture develops paste-like consistency. Add stock and seasonings, cover and simmer on low heat about 30 minutes. Puree in batches in blender or food processor and return to soup kettle. Add heavy cream or half and half and stir until heated through. Serve with a simple salad and crusty bread.

Pineapple-Coconut Bars
Coconut Crust
1/2 cup butter
1 cup firmly packed brown sugar
1-1/2 cups sifted flour
Pinch of salt
1 cup shredded coconut

Filling
2 cups undrained crushed pineapple
6 tablespoons cornstarch
4 tablespoons butter
2 tablespoons lemon juice
1/2 teaspoon salt

Preheat oven to 350 degrees. Cream butter and brown sugar. Blend in flour, salt and coconut until mixture is crumbly. Pat half of mixture into a lightly greased and floured 13x9-inch baking pan. Prepare pineapple filling. Combine pineapple, cornstarch, butter, lemon juice and salt in saucepan. Cook over medium heat, stirring constantly until mixture is thickened and clear. Cool slightly. Pour over crumb layer. Sprinkle remaining crumb mixture on top and press lightly. Bake 30 minutes until slightly browned. Cool and cut into squares.

2

Apple Juice and Classical Music
A duet on the principle of an acquired taste...

Julie's Apple Juice Story

I was not an apple juice fan and never expected to like it, much less have it teach me a valuable lesson. Years ago I had gallstones and learned about an alternative treatment in a book and decided to give it a try. The strategy called for drinking 16 ounces of natural apple juice six times each day for two days. Aside from the apple juice, no other food or liquids were permitted other than water.

After two days of a strict apple juice regimen, I was supposed to take four ounces of virgin olive oil. This treatment created an environment that made it easier for the gallstones to be flushed from the body. To my surprise and delight, it worked! Yet I was even more surprised by the fact that over two days with nothing but apple juice, I started to like it and looked forward to drinking it.

Some things, I discovered, are an acquired taste. Over those two days with no competing food or drink, my palette had made an adjustment...an accommodation of sorts to the fresh, pure taste of apple juice. It's the same way I came to love and enjoy the study of Scripture. At first, it seemed nothing more than words on a page. Along the way, however, I developed a taste for the truth of God's word and ultimately a hunger for God Himself.

Arlene's Classical Music Story

Early in my working life, I kept to a tight morning schedule before leaving home for the hour-long drive to the office. Rock music on the radio accompanied my morning ritual of a quick breakfast, applying make-up and dressing for the day. One morning as I was carefully curling my eyelashes, my radio, for no earthly reason, jumped from the rock station on which it was set to a classical music station a few notches up the dial. I glared at it as if it had gone berserk.

I didn't break my routine though. Taking 20 steps to the kitchen from my dressing table, clearing away the items on the counter in front of the radio, and dialing back to my rock station would eat up precious time I didn't have. The radio was timed to play in the morning only, and I never remembered to adjust it at night.

Weeks later on a snowy morning, I grew increasingly anxious as the minutes ticked by in slow-moving rush hour traffic. Suddenly I became disturbingly aware of my car radio. It seemed to be spewing and belching out the most awful noise and I looked at it…well, as if it had gone berserk. I quickly reached for the dial and scanned over to the soothing, harmonious sounds of my now familiar classical music station. My body and frayed nerves instantly relaxed. It was a "classic" day. A new song had found its way into my heart…much like Christ and His saving grace. Once acquainted, forever changed.

Conversations at the Kitchen Table

- Ask your friends to name one or two things for which they have developed an acquired taste.

- Where does the study of Scripture fall on your "likeability" scale?

- Do these two vignettes encourage you to dust off your Bible and give Scripture a chance?

- Yes? Great…if you're new to the Bible and don't know where to start, begin with the Gospel of John, and then read some of the Apostle Paul's letters to the early churches: Ephesians and Philippians are good ones to start with. Then move on to 1 and 2 Corinthians (the famous "love" quotation read at many wedding ceremonies is from *1 Corinthians 13:4-8*). See, you're already familiar with Scripture! Then check out the book of James, written by the brother of Jesus. Get acquainted with the other Gospels: Matthew, Mark and Luke and follow that up with the Book of Acts. This book tells the story of the Apostles and their journey of faith as they traveled the known world to reach the lost for Christ.

  The Apostle Paul tells the early church in Rome, *"Faith comes from hearing the message, and the message is heard through the word of Christ" (Romans 10:17).* That counsel holds true for us today as well. Reading and meditating on these Scriptures will allow them to begin to take root in your heart, change your attitudes and cause you to think about things in a new way.

  Don't neglect the Old Testament! Psalms and Proverbs are rich and full of wisdom. The book of Ruth is a beautiful portrait of God bringing hope and renewal out of ruins. Read *Isaiah 9:1-7 and chapter 53*, which foretell the coming of Jesus as the Messiah. Now is a good time to find a Bible study group, or form your own, where you can connect with others and discuss what you read, allowing the beauty and wisdom in Scripture to really come alive and catch fire in your heart!

- Let's get better acquainted with the Apostle Paul. We first encounter him as the Pharisee Saul who strongly opposed the early Christians. He believed the followers of Christ were perverting the Jewish faith and was determined to stamp them out. He was on the road to Damascus to arrest more Christians when he had an encounter with the risen Christ. Read *Acts 9.*

  How did Christ personally ordain Saul (renamed Paul) to be His ambassador to the Gentiles? *Acts 9:3-6*

  What does the story say happened to Paul's eyes? *Acts 9:8*

How was Paul's vision restored? *Acts 9:10-18*. This is a graphic illustration of "spiritual blindness." Compare and contrast this illustration with the verse in *1 Corinthians 2:14*.

Lavish "Apple Classic" Lunch

Apples and classical music are the theme for today's "Brunch with Bach!" We found some tasty apple recipes to be enjoyed with a symphony playing in the background! Apples and mustard pair up nicely as a coating for our chicken breasts. Apple crisp is a favorite fall dessert here in Michigan, but it tastes great all year. Here's our friend Rhonda's easy, no-fuss recipe that hands-down beats anything you can purchase at the store.

Apple-Mustard Chicken
4 boneless, skinless chicken breast halves
Salt and pepper
2 tablespoons butter
1/2 cup apple juice
2 tablespoons Dijon mustard

Sprinkle chicken breasts with salt and pepper. In large pan, brown chicken breasts in butter over medium heat three minutes on each side. Stir in apple juice, reduce heat to a simmer and cover. Cook for 10-12 minutes or until chicken is tender and juices run clear, turning once. Remove to a serving plate and keep warm. Add mustard to skillet and whisk in with the apple juice until heated through. Spoon over chicken and serve with a side of steamed veggies.

Rhonda's Apple Crisp
4-5 sliced, peeled apples
1/3 cup sugar
1 teaspoon cinnamon
1/3 cup butter
3/4 cup sifted flour
1/2 cup brown sugar
1/4 cup water
2 teaspoons lemon juice

Preheat oven to 350 degrees. Combine apples, sugar and cinnamon and place in a greased 9x9-inch square pan. Cut the butter into the flour and add sugar, sprinkling over apples. Mix together lemon juice and water and pour into corner of baking dish. Bake 30-40 minutes until apples are tender and crust is golden. Serve with sweetened whipped cream… make your own by beating 1 cup of heavy cream with a little vanilla and powdered sugar until soft peaks form.

3

Handbook for Tourists on Temporary Visas

We're not here for long…five ways to invest in heavenly priorities

❦

"This too shall pass" is a recurrent theme in Scripture. Whatever season or condition of life we find ourselves in…young or old, rich or poor, ill or well, enjoying a season of blessing or coping with a nightmare scenario…it's temporary. Our stay on earth will one day draw to a close.

Many believe that death will be the end of us so our best course is to invest completely in our lives here. Christians, however, know that our eternal home awaits us in glory when we pass from this life. Jesus died to provide us that heavenly passport. We do not qualify for heaven on our own…not by any amount of good deeds or how sterling our characters. The Holy Spirit draws us to Christ who saves us and brings our spirits alive. With changed hearts, we're now empowered to live a life that is pleasing to God. Our faith and trust have to be in Him, not in ourselves. He is the foundation on which we build our spiritual houses. *"For no one can lay any foundation other than the one already laid, which is Jesus Christ" (1 Corinthians 3:11).* As Christians, that's the bedrock from which all of our thought patterns and decisions should arise.

Jesus sets forth these principles in the story of the wise and foolish builders in *Matthew 7:24-27: "Therefore everyone who hears these words of mine and puts them into practice is like a wise man who built his house on the rock. The rain came down, the streams rose, and the winds blew and beat against that house; yet it did not fall, because it has its foundation on the rock. But everyone who hears these words of mine and does not put them into practice is like a foolish man who built his house on sand. The rain came down, the streams rose, and the winds blew and beat against that house, and it fell with a great crash."*

Receiving Christ is a paradigm shift. We're under new management, we have a new assignment and a short time in which to accomplish it: to live a Christ-like life and share the good news of His saving grace to help bring others into the kingdom. Sounds like Mission Impossible, doesn't it? Actually it is. We don't have the chance of a snowball in the inferno of getting this done by ourselves! That's why God sends the Holy Spirit to abide with us as our teacher, guide, helper and comforter. *"…he will give you another Counselor to be with you forever – the Spirit of truth" (John 14:16).*

As members of the Kingdom with a temporary visa for the here and now, we have to look at some things differently so we'll make the best use of our short stay here.

Time – we have a 24-hour gift of time each day that we can either waste on mindless pursuits or spend advancing the kingdom of God. We don't have the endless stretch of days we imagine are ahead of us. *"You are a mist that appears for a little while and then vanishes" (James 4:14).* Paul tells the early church in Corinth that the time is short, and to be careful how they spend their days, *"for this world in its present form is passing away" (1 Corinthians 7:31).* Jesus told his disciples in *John 9:4, "As long as it is day, we must do the work of Him who sent me. Night is coming, when no man can work."* Let's find out what pleases God, and be about His business.

Money – God directs us to bring Him the first fruits of our labor. His investment plan is that we bring him a tenth of all that we earn to our place of worship so that the work of the kingdom can continue. Malachi 3:10, 11 says: *"Bring the whole tithe into the storehouse, that there may be food in my house. 'Test me in this,' says the Lord Almighty, 'and see if I will not throw open the floodgates of heaven and pour out so much blessing that you will not have room for it. I will prevent pests from devouring your crops, and the vines in your fields will not cast their fruit,' says the Lord Almighty."* Give to God what He requires, and He will take care of all our needs.

Thoughts – *"As he thinketh in his heart, so he is" (Proverbs 23:7 KJV).* Our thoughts determine our behavior, our decisions, our actions and ultimately our character and destiny. Spiritually untrained thoughts will naturally follow the flesh and make suppositions, judgments and decisions that do not line up with Scripture. Make God's word the final determination and discard any thoughts or ideas that oppose it. Scripture should serve as our plumb line when thinking through the right way to proceed in any situation. *Proverbs 3:5 says, "Trust in the Lord with all your heart, and lean not on your own understanding."* When we apply our own understanding to any situation against what the Bible instructs, we're headed in the wrong direction.

Activities – *"Above all else, guard your heart, for it is the wellspring of life" (Proverbs 4:23).* Being a Christian increasingly means separating from many of the activities that the world embraces and opting out of a lot of what passes for American culture. Books, TV and movies today offer up a steady stream of violence, graphic language and unbridled sexuality. Witchcraft has undergone a cosmetic makeover in the entertainment world that captivates millions. Satan the deceiver knows how to package sin in attractive, fun, harmless-looking pastimes that entrap those unaware of his schemes. Avoiding these snares and filtering out the flood of muck that confronts us at every turn is a challenge. This is especially true for parents whose children can be so anxious to follow their peers.

Priorities – We seek after many things in life, but the only one that is worthwhile and profitable is to seek God's kingdom. *"But seek first his kingdom and his righteousness, and all*

through us for His will and purpose, *Philippians 2:13*. At the same time, He provides for all of our earthly needs and secures our eternity. *"Do not be afraid, little flock, for your Father has been pleased to give you the kingdom" (Luke 12:32)*. There's just no better deal anywhere on the planet! This doesn't mean we'll avoid heartache, pain, and times of testing and trial. It does mean that we can rest in the assurance of *Romans 8:28: "And we know that in all things God works for the good of those who love him, who have been called according to his purpose."*

- Do you view your life, your possessions, relationships and time as "on loan" from God?

- How would your priorities be altered if you viewed all you had as belonging to God?

- Is your "spiritual house" built on shifting sand or the "rock of Christ?"

- In *Luke 12:16-20*, we read about a rich man who decides to build bigger barns to store his vast array of worldly treasures, then sit back and take life easy. But God says to him, *"You fool! This very night your life will be demanded from you. Then who will get what you have prepared for yourself?"* What other ways could this man have decided to use his worldly goods that would have pleased God and better prepared him for eternity?

- In *Isaiah 58:6-7*, God reveals what pleases Him. *"Is not this the kind of fasting I have chosen: to loose the chains of injustice and untie the cords of the yoke, to set the oppressed free and break every yoke? Is it not to share your food with the hungry and to provide the poor wanderer with shelter-when you see the naked to clothe him and not to turn away from your own flesh and blood?"*

  Make it a point to look around periodically at your family, friends, neighbors, co-workers, and those in your community who could use a helping hand. So many in our midst are lonely and hurting and would be truly blessed by someone dropping off a prepared meal, offering to baby-sit, driving them to an appointment or perhaps inviting them over for a "conversation at the kitchen table!" Don't miss opportunities to "be Jesus" to someone!

- Read *Isaiah 58:8-14*. It lists all of the blessings that God bestows upon those who live such a selfless life!

Lavish "Wayfarer's" Lunch

Today's session has taken us on a tour of a number of spiritual principles that will redirect the course of our lives if we put them into practice. Let's mark this new beginning with a celebration lunch featuring two of our favorite recipes.

Stuffed Jumbo Shells with Spinach and Ricotta

1 package giant shell pasta
1 (8-ounce) package shredded Monterey Jack-cheddar cheese
1 small onion, finely diced
2 garlic cloves, minced
1 package frozen chopped spinach (thaw and squeeze dry)
1 (15 ounce) carton ricotta cheese
1 tablespoon Italian seasoning
2 beaten eggs
Favorite pasta sauce

Preheat oven to 350 degrees. Prepare shell pasta per package directions. In large bowl, combine next seven ingredients. Drain shells and stuff with heaping tablespoon of spinach mixture. Spoon several tablespoons of sauce on bottom of 13x9-inch baking dish. Add stuffed shells and cover with remaining sauce. Bake for 35-40 minutes. Sprinkle with freshly grated Parmesan or mozzarella cheese and serve hearty bread for mopping up sauce.

Chocolate Bread Pudding

4 cups milk
4 (1-ounce) squares unsweetened chocolate, cut up
4 eggs
3/4 cup sugar
1-1/2 teaspoons vanilla
1 cup walnuts, chopped
7-8 cups cubed bread (challah, brioche, French or Italian bread)
Whipped cream for topping
Optional additions: sliced bananas, raspberries, coconut

Preheat oven to 350 degrees. Combine milk and chocolate in a saucepan over medium heat, stirring constantly until melted. Whisk eggs, sugar and vanilla until blended. Whisk in hot chocolate mixture. Stir in nuts and bread until well mixed. Turn batter into a lightly greased 13x9-inch baking dish; spread evenly. Bake uncovered 35-40 minutes or until set. Serve warm with whipped cream.

4

Spiritual Lenses Improve Impaired Vision

What it's like when we don't know Christ

*A*rlene writes…Before I came to faith in Christ, I couldn't see what people who trusted Him were talking about. They spoke of Him with reverence mixed with excitement at the changes He had brought about in their lives. I was raised in a Christian home and knew the Gospel message, but I packed it away in my trunk of childhood memories when I came of age and left home for the adult world. I found other people's faith in Christ terribly sweet in the same way you feel about your best friend who still sleeps with a teddy bear.

How do I describe what that former viewpoint was like now that I have come to faith in Christ? *Isaiah 6:8* calls it *"ever seeing, but never perceiving."* It's a camera lens out of focus, a kaleidoscope that needs one more shift before another image comes forth. It's the blurred vision that our glasses or contacts will correct. It was Helen Keller's state of mind before her gifted teacher broke through her darkness and led her to a world of unimagined light and love.

We just don't realize we lack spiritual lenses. We don't comprehend our fallen natures that separate us from God. Flawed in some areas, sure…but a wicked heart? Never! Scripture, however, tells us otherwise. *"The heart is deceitful above all things and beyond cure. Who can understand it?" (Jeremiah 17:9).* The truths imparted by Scripture can only be "seen" and "heard" by those who have had their eyes and ears spiritually opened. *1 Corinthians 2:14* says, *"The man without the Spirit does not accept the things that come from the Spirit of God, for they are foolishness to him, and he cannot understand them, because they are spiritually discerned."*

This is where "born again" comes in. The Holy Spirit is the only one who can lift the veil from our eyes, where we can see our sin nature grossly revealed against the backdrop of a perfect and holy God. We are finally able to perceive that any "good" we have ever done or think we embody *are like filthy rags" (Isaiah 64:6).* Only then do we realize our need for Christ and His atoning work and our hearts open to receive Him. Then our spirits, quickened by His Spirit, "come alive," and we reengage the world as born again believers. With a new hope, new purpose, and a new set of lenses, we now embark on the day-to-day living out our salvation. The Holy Spirit prompts us to choose new lifestyles, habits and patterns that over time transform us into Christ-likeness.

A popular actor recently stated in an interview, "Life is no dress rehearsal." Actually, it is, and the only one that matters. Life is a boot camp experience… a preparation or practice run that God uses to make us fit for heaven. We come into the world with fallen natures, a condition that only Christ can remedy. God tells us *"be holy, because I am holy" (Leviticus 11:45).* Our transformation from self-absorbed renegades into Christ-likeness begins here on this side of eternity. As with any dress rehearsal, the more we practice, learn our lines and take cues from our Director, the brighter we'll shine on that grand and glorious opening night.

> *"…so that you may become blameless and pure, children of God without fault in a crooked and depraved generation, in which you shine like stars in the universe as you hold out the word of life-in order that I may boast on the day of Christ that I did not run or labor for nothing" (Philippians 2:15, 16).*

Conversations at the Kitchen Table

- Receiving salvation through Christ is not something we do for ourselves on our own initiative. We suffer spiritual blindness until the Holy Spirit opens our eyes and reveals our sinful nature. *"For it is by grace you have been saved, through faith – and this not from yourselves, it is the gift of God – not by works, so that no one can boast" (Ephesians 2:8, 9).*

  What does Jesus say in *John 6:44*?

  What does *2 Corinthians 4:4* reveal about the reason behind our spiritual blindness?

- God draws believers who then receive the salvation Christ offers and are now able to *"participate in the divine nature…" (2 Peter 1:4).* Through them, He makes His appeal to the unsaved world.

  Therefore go and make disciples of all nations, baptizing them in the name of the Father and of the Son and of the Holy Spirit, and teaching them to obey everything I have commanded you (Matthew 28:19-20).

  My prayer is not for them alone. I pray also for those who will believe in me through their message… (John 17:20).

  Always be prepared to give an answer to everyone who asks you to give the reason for the hope that you have (1 Peter 3:15).

- Our mission and focus after receiving salvation is to live a Christ-like life, cultivate a servant's heart, pray for the lost and be ready on every occasion to witness for Christ.

  Discuss living a Christ-like life with your friends by having them read *Colossians 2:1-17.*

  Discuss what it means to be a servant by having your friends read *Luke 19:11-26* where Jesus gives the Parable of the Ten Minas. Ask your friends to identify one way they are investing their lives for Christ.

  Pray for the lost and unsaved of the world whose eyes are blinded to the hope Christ offers.

  Be merciful to those who doubt; snatch others from the fire and save them; to others show mercy, mixed with fear – hating even the clothing stained by corrupted flesh (Jude 23).

Rescue those being led away to death; hold back those staggering toward slaughter. If you say, "But we knew nothing about this," does not he who weighs the heart perceive it? Does not he who guards your life know it? Will he not repay each person according to what he has done? (Proverbs 24:11, 12).

Lavish "New Vision" Lunch

Get a "new vision" for some foods you may not have experienced! We used to avoid both lamb and eggplant until recently. Actually, Julie still does, but I'm working on her! Here's a dish that pairs them nicely.

Lamb with Eggplant-Zucchini Casserole

2 eggplants (1 pound each) cut in 1/2-inch thick rounds
2 medium zucchini, cut into 1/2 inch thick slices
Extra virgin olive oil
1 pound lean ground lamb
1 cup sliced fresh mushrooms
1 cup chopped onion
2 tablespoons finely chopped garlic
1 tablespoon dried oregano
1 tablespoon cumin
Salt and pepper to taste
1 (15-ounce) can diced tomatoes, undrained

Preheat oven to 450 degrees. Brush eggplant and zucchini slices with olive oil and place on a baking sheet and roast 15-20 minutes until tender. Remove and reduce oven to 375 degrees. Meanwhile, sauté lamb, draining off excess liquid. Add mushrooms, onions and garlic and sauté another few minutes. Quarter eggplant and zucchini slices and add to lamb mixture along with tomatoes and seasonings. Spoon into a 13 x 9-inch casserole dish and bake 25-30 minutes.

Pineapple-Angel Food Cake

1 package angel food cake mix
1 (15-ounce) can crushed pineapple with juice
2 cups homemade or purchased whipped cream

Preheat oven to 350 degrees. Combine cake mix with can of crushed pineapple, undrained. Bake in a 13x9-inch baking dish for 40-45 minutes until golden. Cool and serve with whipped cream. An additional can of crushed pineapple can be added; however, **drain** this one well before adding to cake batter.

5

Don't Run Your Own Railroad

Mapping out our own plans leads to disappointment and regret

rlene writes…"Run your own railroad," was a favorite expression of a long-time friend of mine. He believes we need to take charge of our lives and steer our own courses. It's a popular notion, especially in America where we pride ourselves on our independence and celebrate it every Fourth of July. We're trained to believe greatness lies with those who are masters of their own destinies. Most conventional wisdom like this, however, gets turned on its head in God's Kingdom.

We want to call our own shots, make our own decisions, and be in the driver's seat, yet God created us to be dependent upon Him. Jesus tells us in *John 15:5, "I am the vine, you are the branches. If a man remains in me and I in him, he will bear much fruit; apart from me you can do nothing."* We think we can, however, and merrily map out plans, chart our own courses and live entirely apart from God's will, purpose and plan for our lives. Then decades later, most of us lament that our lives fell miles short of our youthful aspirations and wonder where it all went wrong. Those who did achieve everything they desired are left wondering what else they need to accomplish to fill the emptiness in their souls.

Does God really have a plan for each of our lives? In *Jeremiah 29:11*, we read, *"For I know the plans I have for you,"* declares the Lord, *"plans to prosper you and not to harm you, plans to give you hope and a future."* He designed each one of us with our own personal unique characteristics and equipped us with specific gifts, talents and abilities … so that we could stumble around and hit the skids? Puh-leeze! Read *Psalm 139:13-16, "For you created my inmost being; you knit me together in my mother's womb. I praise you because I am fearfully and wonderfully made; your works are wonderful, I know that full well. My frame was not hidden from you when I was made in the secret place. When I was woven together in the depths of the earth, your eyes saw my unformed body."* That should cause us all to sit up and take notice! His plan for us doesn't stop there, and He wants us to walk it out with Him. But He'll never force it on us. He's given us free will, and we have to choose to follow Him or walk our own way.

His plan is far superior to anything we can try to accomplish on our own. We may think that so far we've done just fine without the Lord's involvement - which is kind of silly when we consider that God is sovereign, omnipotent and omnipresent while we, on the other hand, have the barest sliver of knowledge and wisdom to guide us. In *Jeremiah 2:13*, God says, "*'My people have committed two sins: They have forsaken me, the spring of living water, and have dug their own cisterns, broken cisterns that cannot hold water.'*"

Wisdom calls for turning over the reins to our loving Heavenly Father who appeals to us in *Isaiah 55:1-3*, "*Come, all you who are thirsty, come to the waters; and you who have no money, come, buy and eat! Come, buy wine and milk without money and without cost. Why spend money on what is not bread, and your labor on what does not satisfy? Listen, listen to me, and eat what is good, and your soul will delight in the richest of fare. Give ear and come to me; hear me that your soul may live.*"

- Are you still running your own railroad?

- Do you trust God enough to let Him be the engineer?

- Read and review the following passages that make it clear that God wants to run our railroads.

  What causes God to weep in secret? See *Jeremiah 13:15-17*.

  What is the result of not listening and heeding His direction? See *Isaiah 48:17-19*.

  What are the benefits of paying attention to God's commands? See *Proverbs 3:5, 6*.

  What will God do when we acknowledge Him in our ways?

- Ask your friends to describe an experience or situation they could not control. Were they able to see God's hand in its resolution? If not, and they are still suffering the repercussions, pray with them and ask God to pick up the pieces and bring about resolution.

- It's never too late to ask for God's intervention even if years or decades have taken us far from our intended path. Read *Joel 2:25*. What does it say about the promise of God to restore lives that have been ravaged? Use this passage to reassure your friends that the Lord's promise to restore them is faithful and true!

"When I said, 'My foot is slipping,' your love, O Lord, supported me. When anxiety was great within me, your consolation brought joy to my soul" (Psalm 94:18, 19).

Arlene rode the rails often as a young girl when her dad worked for a railroad. Her first "lavish lunches" were experienced in the club cars of express trains speeding across the country. Here's an offering she would love to find on the menu!

Our Favorite Crockpot Stew
2-3 tablespoons olive oil
1 pound boneless beef top round
1 (32-ounce) carton of organic beef broth
2 potatoes, peeled and diced
2 stalks celery, sliced
1 onion, cut into 1/4-inch slices
1 (15-ounce) can Northern beans
2 cups frozen organic mixed vegetables (carrots, peas, corn, and green beans)
1 teaspoon each basil, tarragon, rosemary and thyme
Salt and pepper to taste
2 tablespoons flour or cornstarch
1/4 cup water

Trim fat from beef and cut into pieces. In a large skillet coated with olive oil, brown beef on both sides over medium-high heat. Place in slow cooker along with next nine ingredients. Cover and cook on low temperature 7-8 hours or until meat is tender. To thicken stew, stir in a mixture of flour or cornstarch and water switching temperature back to high for 10-12 minutes. Serve with crusty bread or rolls.

Carrot-Zucchini Bars
1 cup butter, softened
1 cup brown sugar
2 eggs
1 teaspoon vanilla
1 cup grated zucchini (wrung dry)
1 cup grated carrots
1-3/4 cups whole-wheat flour
1-1/2 teaspoons baking powder
1 cup rolled oats
1/2 cup ground flaxseed
1 cup chopped walnuts
1/2 cup powdered sugar
2-3 tablespoons milk

Preheat oven to 350 degrees. In a medium bowl, cream together butter, sugar, eggs and vanilla. Stir in zucchini and carrots. In separate bowl, mix together flour, baking powder, oats and ground flaxseed. Stir dry ingredients into the creamed mixture and fold in the nuts. Spread into a lightly greased 13x9-inch pan. Bake 30-35 minutes. Combine powdered sugar and milk and drizzle lightly over cooled crust. Cut into squares or diamonds.

6

Trouble – Nowhere to Run, Nowhere to Hide

Trouble is guaranteed: take a couple of Psalms and meet us for lunch

With or without Christ in our lives, trouble is guaranteed, so better to face it with Him. Christ gives us the bad news and the good news in the same breath, *"In this world you will have trouble. But take heart! I have overcome the world" (John 16:33).* Trouble is our opportunity to put God's word into practice and see His power displayed in our lives. Facing trials strengthens our spiritual muscles and deepens our trust in God. It's worth remembering that all sunshine makes a desert. Nothing grows without rain, and neither would we if our lives were filled with unending sunshine.

Yet trouble can smash our hearts and make us bitter if we try to handle it alone. In the midst of the storms, we have to learn to take God at His word: *"Do not let your hearts be troubled. Trust in God, trust also in me" (John 14:1).* Unless we have some practice at handling trouble using spiritual principles, we'll never be able to trust His promises to cover and sustain us. *"'Though the mountains be shaken and the hills be removed, yet my unfailing love for you will not be shaken nor my covenant of peace be removed,' says the Lord, who has compassion on you" (Isaiah 54:10).*

Christ never calls us to do anything He did not do. His anguish in the Garden of Gethsemane caused Him to sweat great drops of blood. See *Luke 22:44.* Our Lord knows what it's like to face heartache, pain, betrayal – so who better to trust when we encounter these things? *"He was despised and rejected by men, a man of sorrows, and familiar with suffering" (Isaiah 53:3).* By faith and prayer, He prepared Himself to lay down His life to vanquish sin for all time. As His followers, we will reap glory from His sacrifice, but as His followers, we will come up against our share of trouble and suffering as well. *1 Peter 4:13* tells us *"Rejoice that you participate in the sufferings of Christ, so that you may be overjoyed when his glory is revealed."*

In ways we don't understand, suffering accomplishes a great work in us when we trust God with it. Our natural selves are willful, stubborn and contrary to God's will. The blacksmith's hammer shapes pieces of iron into useful objects. Pain and hardship shape us into what we would never become otherwise. All of us would opt out of suffering if we could. Yet it is an essential ingredient the Lord can use to mold, shape, and train us to handle everything in His strength, not ours.

Christ set the example of praying through every step of His earthly life and ministry. Since He found it necessary, how could we not? Follow His lead, child of God. Much is accomplished if we don't panic, freak out, break down, run away, become a basket case, sink into despair, turn to drugs, abuse alcohol, lose our faith and decide that God has abandoned us. Scripture tells us that it will take painful situations and circumstances in order for us to be transformed into the glorious likeness of Christ. *"Therefore we do not lose heart. Though outwardly we are wasting away, yet inwardly we are being renewed day by day. For our light and momentary troubles are achieving for us an eternal glory that far outweighs them all (2 Corinthians 4:16, 17).*

"I saw the angel in the marble and carved until I set him free." Michelangelo

- Have you encountered troubling situations and circumstances that have caused you anxiety and sleepless nights? Have you suffered bouts of fear and depression?

- Have these trials prompted you to call on God and seek guidance in His word?

- If so, have these episodes served to strengthen your faith and enable you to counsel others going through a similar crisis? Sometimes this is the very reason God has us experience difficulties. *"Praise be to the God and Father of our Lord Jesus Christ, the Father of compassion and the God of all comfort, who comforts us in all our troubles, so that we can comfort those in any trouble with the comfort we ourselves have received from God"* (2 Corinthians 1:3, 4).

- Ask your friends to look back at a past trial and identify how it was instrumental in helping them to grow. If anyone is unable to find the good in a trial, read *2 Corinthians 4:7-18* and pray with them.

"The Lord himself goes before you and will be with you; He will never leave you nor forsake you. Do not be afraid; do not be discouraged" (Deuteronomy 31:8).

"When I said, 'My foot is slipping,' your love, O Lord, supported me. When anxiety was great within me, your consolation brought joy to my soul" (Psalm 94:18, 19).

Since trouble is a guarantee, we need to keep ourselves strong and fit with a supply of muscle-building, starch-in-the-spine recipes at the ready. This hearty lentil soup is nutritious and satisfying! These oatmeal-date bars were Arlene's mom's specialty, and they were featured at almost every family gathering.

Lentil Soup
1 cup lentils
1 cup brown rice
1 small onion, chopped
2 stalks celery, chopped
2 cups frozen organic mixed vegetables
1 can diced tomatoes
1 (15-ounce) can white beans, drained
1 small can tomato sauce
1 (32-ounce) carton organic chicken broth
1 tablespoon cumin
1 tablespoon dried basil
1 tablespoon dried oregano
Salt and pepper to taste

Combine all ingredients in a soup kettle and bring to a boil. Cover and lower heat to a simmer for 30-40 minutes. Add water if soup is too thick, adjust seasonings and continue to simmer for additional 10-15 minutes. Serve with crusty bread and a mixed green salad.

Mom's Date-filled Oatmeal Bars
Crust
2 cups quick-cooking oats
1 cup brown sugar
2 cups flour
1/4 teaspoon salt
1 teaspoon baking soda
1 cup butter, softened
1 egg
1 teaspoon vanilla

Filling
1 pound of fresh dates, chopped
1 cup sugar
1 cup water

Preheat oven to 350 degrees. In a medium saucepan, combine filling ingredients, bring to a boil, and then lower to a simmer for 10 minutes. Meanwhile, combine oats, brown sugar, flour, salt, soda and softened butter. Beat egg with vanilla and add to mixture using your carefully washed hands to thoroughly mix ingredients. Press half of mixture into buttered 13x9-inch pan. Spoon the date sauce over pastry and top with reserved oat mixture. Bake 30 minutes. Cool and cut into bars.

7

I Will Be With You Always

We may not always feel His presence, but He's right by our side

⁓

The last words Jesus gave to His disciples before He ascended to Heaven were, *"And surely I am with you always, to the very end of the age" (Matthew 28:20).* That promise extends to all of us who have received the gift of salvation Christ freely offers.

Why then do we sometimes feel alone and abandoned? The promise Jesus gave is indeed true because the *"Scripture cannot be broken" (John 10:35)* and *"God is not a man that he should lie" (Numbers 23:19).* But that doesn't mean that we will always feel His presence. Sometimes it seems as if God falls silent in our darkest hours. His purpose in these seasons is to develop our faith and grow us into *"oaks of righteousness" (Isaiah 61:3)* that the fiercest storms cannot wither, crack, break or uproot. *"We live by faith, not by sight," (2 Corinthians 5:7)* knowing that He will never go back on His promise to be with us.

Many titles are ascribed to Jesus as our Lord, but perhaps the most tender and familiar is His depiction as The Good Shepherd in *John 10:11.* As a shepherd moves his sheep to the higher elevations on the mountain for the best grazing, Jesus calls us to come higher with Him. Throughout this ascent, however, the sheep face mountain lions, wolves, jagged cliffs, steep terrain, flash floods and raging storms that completely envelop them in darkness. They don't always see or sense the shepherd, yet he is always on the job looking out for their safety, and he knows instantly when one of them is attacked, stumbles, or loses its way.

So too with us. Jesus is aware of every battle, every failure, every crisis and heartbreak that befalls us. Even when we don't see or sense His presence, we are to keep climbing because Scripture tells us, *"The righteous will live by faith" (Romans 1:17).* At its very core, faith is unwavering certainty in the promises of God even when they are not yet manifest. Now *"faith is being sure of what we hope for and certain of what we do not see" (Hebrews 11:1).* As the Good Shepherd, He is working behind the scenes, up ahead and out of our sight range. He is clearing our path, pulling up bitter roots in our hearts, freeing us from the entanglements of the wilderness, and keeping us from the mouth of Satan, our ever-present adversary, who lies in wait *"to steal and kill and destroy ..." (John 10:10).*

Through His word, He continually beckons, calls and urges us to climb higher to the rarified atmosphere of the heavenly realms. When the storm clouds block the sun, when the steep terrain threatens to topple us, when the darkness is so black we cannot see the way, we must hold fast to the promise of Jesus to sustain us. *"Even though I walk through the valley of the shadow of death, I will fear no evil, for you are with me" (Psalm 23:4).* When it feels as if we're completely alone in our struggle, He is waiting to rendezvous with us in Scripture where His word serves as *"a lamp to my feet and a light for my path" (Psalm 119:105).*

Conversations at the Kitchen Table

- Is there a trial you or one of your friends is facing that seems too big to handle? Our natural reactions are to first seek our own remedies, but we are to *"come boldly to the throne of grace, that we may obtain mercy, and find grace to help in time of need"* (Hebrews 4:16).

- Whatever the situation, there are Scriptures that address the situation. Read and discuss the following passages with your friends:
  Psalm 27
  Psalm 46
  Psalm 91
  Psalm 119:97-102
  Psalm 119:145-152
  Psalm 121

- Bring these Scriptures before the Lord in your prayer time and ask for His guidance and counsel in dealing with your struggle. Trust Him to bring about the resolution and hold fast to His promises.

- Can you identify signs that God is at work on your problem? If that's not yet apparent, are you holding fast to the promise and resting in His peace? Christ said *"Peace I leave with you; my peace I give you. I do not give to you as the world gives"* (John 14:27).

  "Cast your cares on the Lord and he will sustain you; He will never let the righteous fall" (Psalm 55:22).

  "Your path led through the sea, your way through the mighty waters, though your footprints were not seen" (Psalm 77:19).

Lavish "Everlasting Presence" Lunch

Several of Jesus' disciples were fishermen, see *Matthew 4:18, 19*. We think they would have liked this dish! Try our dessert with the whimsical title. While we usually think of angels as delicate and pristine, they are warriors. *"Praise the Lord, you his angels, you mighty ones..."* *(Psalm 103:20).* Even if they have occasion to get muddy on our behalf, they always emerge victorious!

Parmesan-Sour Cream Fish Bake
1-1/2 to 2 pounds cod, haddock or tilapia
1 cup sour cream
1/4 cup grated Parmesan cheese
1 tablespoon lemon juice
1/2 teaspoon salt
1 tablespoon grated onion if desired
Paprika
Fresh parsley

Preheat oven to 350 degrees. Place fish in lightly greased baking dish. Combine rest of ingredients, coat fish and finish with a dusting of paprika and parsley. Bake 30 minutes or until fish flakes easily with a fork. Serve with seasoned red skin potatoes.

Angel-in-the Mud Cake
1 package angel food cake mix
1 package organic chocolate pudding
1-1/2 cups heavy cream or purchased whipped cream

Prepare and bake angel food cake according to package directions. Prepare chocolate pudding. When cake is cooled, break into pieces and scatter in a 13x9-inch casserole dish. Pour pudding over angel cake pieces. Beat whipping cream until soft peaks form. Spoon and spread evenly over pudding and cake. Chill, then serve with additional whipped cream.

8

Knowing Who We Are In Christ
The bedrock of self-esteem

Arlene writes… A friend of mine used to call me an extremist. I thought he was off base, but it turns out he was dead right in his assessment. I was given to manic-depressive episodes on a fairly regular basis. One day I was a priceless jewel wrapped in a gold setting, destined for great things; the next day lower than a snake's belly, wondering if I was even capable of running a lemonade stand.

One of my short stories won a writing competition in college…I'm on top of the world; my work project received harsh reviews…I'm on the dark side of the moon. A boyfriend sent flowers…up; he didn't call for a week…down. My boss sang my praises at a staff meeting…high fives; the stylist cut my hair too short…plunged into a pit. My friends throw a surprise birthday party…wildly happy; a loved one breaks a trusted confidence…mortified and depressed.

My sense of worth and value fluctuated like the Dow Jones Industrial Average. There was no even keel, no set point at which I could operate and not get thrown like the last one in line at a game of crack-the-whip. One day I was like a peacock with colored feathers on glorious display, the next day shriveled in a corner like a lost, torn package at the post office with no address. The loser/useless/worthless audiotape would channel up and bombard my brain with a negative blast, rewinding itself over and over until I sank under heavy conviction. Then surprisingly, I would experience something wonderful and the loser audiotape would eject, replaced by an equally ridiculous "unstoppable/hear me roar/can't touch this" tape. And I let myself get played. You'd think it would wear a girl out. Well, it finally did.

One day I hit a wall and couldn't recover. I crumbled over a job assignment that was outside my skill set. I'm a writer, not a project manager. I soon got lost in the overwhelming amount of detail and follow-up required and had a full-blown meltdown. At first, I couldn't sleep…then my appetite went south and I couldn't eat. In a month, I'd dropped 20 pounds, my clothes hung on me, I was becoming incoherent, co-workers began whispering, and my family and friends were horrified at the zombie-like state into which I sank. I went on a medical leave to try and recover. There are a variety of names for this condition: clinical depression, post-traumatic stress disorder, hopelessness, despair.

The "loser" audiotape played incessantly. There were no manic recovery episodes on the horizon to counter this crash, and my hard shell of self-sufficiency and "fake it 'til we make it" modus operandi collapsed around me. This was humpty-dumpty in full-scale plummet, and no king's army was going to put it back together again. That is until the King Himself stepped in...the King of Kings and the Lord of Lords. In my panic and despair, I cried out for help and He heard me. Or shall I say, I could finally hear Him? While I trusted Christ as my Savior, I had been too busy running my own railroad.

"The Lord is close to the brokenhearted and saves those who are crushed in spirit" (Psalm 34:18). For some of us, a crash-and-burn episode is the only time God gets our attention. We exclude him with our hard, crusty exterior shells of self-sufficiency. He will not trespass our fenced off property and the "do not enter" signs at our gate. His only chance to cross our threshold is when we're at a place of brokenness. Then He has a chance to enter in, but not like a looter looking to raid damaged property and pick off our possessions. He comes to give us an even greater possession: Himself. And with Him comes peace to calm the storm, gentleness to soothe a ravaged soul, hope to revive a barely-beating heart, love to bind our wounds and nail-scarred hands that lift us gently to our feet.

He doesn't scold us for the mess He encounters either, just walks us out of the cellar, opens the windows to allow for the fresh breeze of the Holy Spirit, pours steel reinforcement into our shaky frames and rebuilds our house upon the rock instead of quicksand. He trashes both the "I am a loser / I am invincible" tapes replacing them with *"I can do everything through him who gives me strength" (Philippians 4:13),* a message that settles once and for all who we really are: children of the Living God, separated apart and made holy by His blood, called forth to show His glory. That's a set point we can return to again and again when we're thrown. That's an identity in which we can place our confidence even when we fail. That's an address that's permanent no matter how many times we move. That's true north on the compass. That's an anchor that holds in any storm-tossed sea. That's what defines us, balances our equilibrium, gives us our sense of worth and value, and frees us from fear, dread and the opinions of others.

Knowing who we are in Christ is the bedrock of self-esteem. Without it, we'll spend far too many days evaluating our worth and value by the standards of this world, one that judges according to the most transient and superficial of traits: whether we have fat bank accounts or clip coupons; whether we look like super models or the bride of Frankenstein; whether we're fashionably thin or comfortably padded; have Ph.D.s or room-temperature IQs; are young and strong or aged and frail; married well or not at all; have smart kids or ones who need tutors; live in the right zip code or the wrong side of the tracks.

None of these traits and conditions qualify to serve as any kind of barometer against which to judge our worth and value. They don't define our characters and our hearts, the two things that matter to God. We are created in His image, and we have value to Him for that reason alone. Nothing can change that, for *"Who shall separate us from the love of Christ? Shall trouble or hardship or persecution or famine or nakedness or danger or sword? ...No, in all these things we are more than conquerors through him who loved us" (Romans 8:35, 37).*

Once we know that we matter to God and that He loves us unconditionally, we'll never again be so tightly tethered to the world's system. No seismic shift in circumstances that flattens us like a pancake or passing star that snags our coat and rockets us to transient glory will

who loves us and has called us His own.

> *"Why should you be beaten anymore? Why do you persist in rebellion? Your whole head is injured, your whole heart afflicted. From the sole of your feet to the top of your head, there is no soundness – only wounds and welts and open sores, not cleansed or bandaged or soothed with oil." (Isaiah 1:5, 6)*

> *"I am the way and the truth and the life" (John 14:6).*

- Are you relying on your own strength and self-sufficiency to guide you through life?

- Has your self-esteem ever cracked and left you wondering who you are?

- Is your worth and value based on things that can disappear overnight?

- How does knowing who you are in Christ make life more manageable and give it meaning?

For he will deliver the needy who cry out, the afflicted who have no one to help. He will take pity on the weak and the needy and save the needy from death. He will rescue them from oppression and violence, for precious is their blood in his sight (Psalm 72:12-14).

His divine power has given us everything we need for life and godliness through our knowledge of him who called us by his own glory and goodness (2 Peter 1:3).

Lavish "Swing for the Fences" Lunch

Knowing who we are in Christ puts us in play as a power hitter! Let's swing for the fences by combining today's message with a serving of spinach… always on hand in our kitchens. We love pumpkin treats all year around, not just for Thanksgiving. Arlene's sister Denise makes her pumpkin pie with Stevia (found in upscale markets and health food stores in powdered packets or liquid form) and ground flaxseed for a healthy taste treat you can feel good about serving!

Spinach Stuffed Chicken Breasts
4 boneless, skinless chicken breast halves
1 (10-ounce) package frozen, chopped spinach (thaw and squeeze dry)
1 (4-ounce) package crumbled feta cheese
1 beaten egg
1 (15-ounce) jar Alfredo sauce

Cover chicken breasts with waxed paper and pound with a heavy pan to flatten. Combine spinach, feta and egg, placing two tablespoons on one half of each chicken breast and fold over. Transfer breasts to lightly greased casserole dish. Spoon alfredo sauce over each breast. Bake at 350 degrees for 35-40 minutes.

Denise's Revved-Up Pumpkin Pie
1 unbaked pie crust
1 teaspoon cinnamon
1/2 teaspoon ginger
1/4 teaspoon cloves
3 packets powdered Stevia (a natural non-caloric, sweet-tasting alternative to sugar)
1/4 cup ground flaxseed
2 large eggs
1 (15-ounce) can pumpkin
1 (12-ounce) can evaporated milk

Preheat oven to 425 degrees. Combine spices, Stevia and flaxseed. Beat eggs separately, and then stir in pumpkin and spice mixture. Gradually stir in evaporated milk. Pour into pie shell. Bake at 425 degrees for 15 minutes, then lower temperature to 350 degrees and bake additional 40-50 minutes or until toothpick inserted in pie center comes out clean. Cool and serve with whipped cream.

9

My Pregnancy Center Adventure
Julie helps establish a pregnancy center

*J*ulie writes…Years ago I was one of the founders of a crisis pregnancy center in Wixom, Michigan. I worked with a handful of women to bring the pregnancy center into being. Six of us were involved in various tasks: finding a name, researching appropriate bylaws, completing incorporation papers, networking with community resource agencies, and finding a suitable location for our facility.

We wanted to create a place where women would feel confident their situations would be kept confidential, they would be treated with respect, and they would get honest help. We offered free pregnancy tests and peer counseling services. If a client was single and not pregnant, we wanted to provide her with information that would help her make better choices in the future about having sex outside marriage. If she was pregnant and unmarried, we offered parenting and adoption options and worked with her as she decided what was best for her and her baby. If she was married, we helped her and often her husband as well with plans to make having a new baby financially viable.

To develop the financial support for our center, we invited pastors and their staffs from all the local churches. About 10 people came to our first meeting. Some made financial contributions that evening, and others wanted to find out more about it before committing. Many were interested in how we planned to encourage the girls and women to come to the center in the first place. We explained that we would place ads in the Yellow Pages, local newspapers and church bulletins.

In the formative years as the center was gaining recognition in the community, the churches represented potential referrals, donors and a source for volunteers. We found community resources for the services our clients would need: a government nutrition program called Women, Infants and Children, a clothes closet that had infant and maternity clothing as well as baby furniture, formula and diapers, doctors who would see our clients free or inexpensively, and residential programs and homes for younger women who would be forced to leave home if they carried a baby to term. Eventually we had a big clothes and baby formula closet of our own.

We joined Pregnancy Services of Michigan, a coalition of pregnancy centers throughout the state. The field director of the coalition came and taught us listening and caring skills. We developed a Bible-based training program for our volunteers.

We planned an open house for the first Sunday in November 1984. People from churches that partnered with us, our friends and families, those who saw our announcement in the paper, all showed up that day. So did our first client. I was concerned that we would open our doors and no one would come! Now we had our first client, and a day early!

The center is still serving the community, although I haven't been physically involved for ten years. I was president and eventually director for the first ten years. Now others have taken the helm, and the center marked its 21st anniversary in November, 2005.

Without a doubt, my ten years with the center were some of the happiest of my life. I had to depend so much on God at the time with decisions that would impact many lives. When I wasn't sure which way to go, I would pray and proceed along a particular pathway until it became clear whether or not that was the right choice. I believe that is God's way. He likes to give us the next step, but rarely displays the entire picture at once. It certainly keeps us from getting out too far ahead of Him and makes the adventure more exciting!

Abortion is common in our world and we all know family members, friends and others who have taken this step. It may be presented as a quick fix, but much heartache, regret and a sense of loss invariably settles in down the road. Even when our poor choices and bad judgment land us in a mess, and we see no other way out, God has a plan. We urge any woman facing this dilemma or who is in a position to advise and counsel someone weighing this option to seek out a facility like Another Way Pregnancy Center to consider other options that will lead to new life.

If you've had an abortion, ask for God's forgiveness and then forgive yourself. Many women find peace by becoming counselors to help others sort through this difficult issue. Others join in walk-for-life fundraisers for a pregnancy clinic or volunteer at their church to care for young children while their mothers take Bible studies. There are a number of avenues that will help you to affirm life, nurture children, support young families and find the peace so many women seek in the aftermath of an abortion. Remember that God loves us with an everlasting love. Nothing can separate us from His love!

> *"For God did not send his Son into the world to condemn the world, but to save the world through him" (John 3:17).*

> *"His compassions never fail. They are new every morning..." (Lamentations 3:22, 23).*

There's a bit more prep work to this dish, but it's worth the effort! Reward yourself with Berry-Chocolate Supreme and expect raves from your guests!

Very Veggie Lasagna
2 cups organic broccoli florets
2 cups organic cauliflower florets
2 organic carrots, sliced
2 small zucchini, quartered and cut into 1/2 inch slices
1 cup sliced mushrooms
2 jars favorite pasta sauce
1 (15-ounce) carton part-skim ricotta cheese
1 (15-ounce) carton cottage cheese
2 beaten eggs
1 (8-ounce) package shredded mozzarella
2 teaspoons Italian seasoning
1 package no-boil lasagna noodles

Preheat oven to 350 degrees. Steam broccoli, cauliflower and carrots for 4 minutes. Place in large mixing bowl. Add zucchini and mushrooms. Combine beaten eggs and cheeses and fold into veggie mixture. Spoon two tablespoons pasta sauce into bottom of a 13x9-inch casserole dish. Add layer of lasagna noodles. Top with half of the veggie cheese mixture, then cover with half the pasta sauce. Repeat layers. Top with additional mozzarella. Bake at 350 degrees for 45-50 minutes. Let stand for 15 minutes before slicing. Serve with garlic toast and green salad.

Berry-Chocolate Supreme
Crust
2 cups flour
1/2 cup powdered sugar
1/2 cup butter, melted

Topping
1 cup raspberry preserves
4 ounces white chocolate chips, melted
1 (3-ounce) package cream cheese
2 squares unsweetened chocolate
1 tablespoon butter

Preheat oven to 350 degrees. Mix crust ingredients together and press into 9x9-inch baking dish. Bake for 15 minutes. Spread berry preserves over cooled crust. Melt white chocolate chips and cool slightly before beating with cream cheese. Drop cheese in dollops over berry topping. Use a spatula to cover cake. Melt together unsweetened chocolate and butter and drizzle over cheese topping. Cover and chill; bring to room temperature before serving.

10

The Women of Another Way Pregnancy Center
Women helping women in the throes of crisis

*J*ulie writes…In the early start-up days of Another Way Pregnancy Center, we were staffed solely by a group of volunteers. Within a few years, we had enough support to have two paid staff people.

Women of all ages, income levels, and church denominations made up our volunteer staff, and nearly all were associated with a church. Some had abortion backgrounds themselves and wanted the opportunity to advise other women not to make the same mistake. Abortion can easily be presented as a quick fix to an unexpected problem. Over the course of time, however, many of these women grieved their loss and desperately wanted to counsel others not to make a decision that would bring similar regrets. They made themselves available to offer their own "been there/done that" experience to those facing the same dilemma.

The women who came to the center as clients fell into three main age groups, 14-18, 19-23, and 24 and older. The largest group was the 19-23 year old group. These women often believed the lie that having sex was a sign of maturity; a modern rite of passage, the primary means of demonstrating love for their boyfriends. Many were pressured for sex and were anxious to please in order not to lose them. Now that they suspected they were pregnant, they were extremely concerned how the pregnancy test turned out, realizing how their jobs, college and careers would be affected now and in the future.

Some women brought their boyfriends along with them. Some men were supportive, while others came along to manipulate their girlfriends in favor of a quick end to the "problem." For these men, there was no desire to bring these babies into the world. That was our recommendation, except in the case where the woman's life was endangered by carrying the child. It was important and helpful to us to talk to the couple together and then to speak to each one separately. Then we could see if there really was consensus in how they perceived the situation.

The 14-18 year old group concerned us the most. These girls seemed so much like victims to us, even though they weren't able to see it that way. They often were dating much older men who professed love for them, but had no intention of accompanying them down this road of unintended consequences. We were successful in changing the minds of about half the women of all ages who were considering abortion. While it was our desire to convince all to avoid abortion, we were grateful to have a 50/50 track record.

I valued every moment of the ten years God placed me in service at the pregnancy center, first as president and later as center director. I learned a great deal about human nature, and especially about women who undervalue their worth and fall prey to the affections of men who don't have their best interests at heart. Our self-esteem and self-worth are based on knowing who we are in Christ. The earlier we understand that, the more likely we are to avoid the pitfalls of contemporary society that tells us it's based on our income, worldly achievements, the man at our side or some other outward display.

We need to let Christ rule and reign in our hearts, and He will help to refocus our vision to our true identities. Let's teach our young women about what wonders we truly are, how unique we are in individuality and talent, reflecting the very image of the Creator Himself!

- Do you see that God, rather than looking to spoil your fun, designed sexual expression within the confines of marriage to protect you and keep you from damaging your life?

- Is it clear by now that a man who truly loves you and is committed to you wants to protect you and provide a haven for you within marriage rather than trying to convince you to hook up with him for momentary pleasure?

- Is your self-esteem based on knowing who you are in Christ or outward displays like the man at your side, the size of your bank account or the zip code you live in – all of which are subject to change?

- Are you allowing your values and standards to be set by the current culture or God's decrees? He desires your best even if it seems His ways are narrow and stringent.

As the heavens are higher than the earth, so are my ways higher than your ways and my thoughts than your thoughts (Isaiah 55:9).

Taste and see that the Lord is good; blessed is the man who takes refuge in Him. Fear the Lord, you his saints, for those who fear him lack nothing. The lions may grow weak and hungry, but those who seek the Lord lack no good thing (Psalm 34:8-10).

The Holy Spirit is our best coach and counselor, but so are other women who have walked the road before us. Perhaps you could invite one or two of them over for this lavish lunch!

Pumpkin Chowder
1 (32-ounce) carton organic chicken broth
1 (20-ounce) can of pumpkin
2 cups heavy cream or half-and-half
1 package frozen, organic vegetables (broccoli, cauliflower and carrots)
1 teaspoon tarragon
1 teaspoon oregano
Salt and pepper

Steam organic vegetables four minutes, cutting any large pieces into smaller sizes. In a large soup kettle, combine chicken broth, pumpkin, steamed vegetables and seasonings. Add cream, stirring until heated through.

Cranberry-Apricot Bars
Crust
1 cup flour
1/3 cup brown sugar
1/2 cup butter, melted

Filling
1/3 cup golden raisins
1/2 cup dried cranberries
1/2 cup chopped dried apricots
1 cup water

Topping
2 eggs
1 cup brown sugar
1/2 cup flour
1 teaspoon vanilla
1/3 cup chopped nuts
Powdered sugar

Preheat oven to 350 degrees. Combine raisins, cranberries and apricots in water and bring to boil in saucepan. Remove from heat and let stand 20 minutes before draining. Meanwhile, make crust by mixing flour, brown sugar and melted butter and press into lightly greased 8 or 9-inch baking pan. Bake for 20 minutes. Beat eggs on low speed for 3-4 minutes. Stir in brown sugar, flour and vanilla. Add fruit, nuts and pour evenly over crust. Bake 40 minutes. Cool and sprinkle with powdered sugar.

11

Encounter With Elephants...
A Safari without Leaving Home
Finding your way with like companions

*A*rlene writes...Before I became a Christian, I attended a seminar for children of alcoholics. I thought that by excavating my past I would uncover some clues to my inability to create a satisfying life. Two simple exercises were held outdoors. The first called for half the group to form a circle facing inward with their eyes closed. The other half of the group was to move around the outside of the circle stopping behind each person to whisper words of endearment and encouragement: you are loved, you are highly prized, you will have a wonderful, successful life, you are a magnificent creation and a wonderful gift to those around you, and so on.

Hearing these sweet, loving words whispered by someone who gently held our arms or shoulders was like a soothing balm poured over our restless, troubled spirits. These whispered affirmations could have been the parent that always seemed distant and remote...or someone in our lives we wished loved us now...or the promise of a future someone who one day would provide us with the unconditional love we so longed for.

In the second activity we were to identify an animal we really liked. With eyes closed, we moved about the group making the sound of our chosen animal while listening for similar sounds to find those of our kind. Some chose cats, dogs, horses, and I remember choosing an elephant. I had no clue what kind of sound an elephant makes, so I moved through the group whispering "Elephants...any elephants here?" And, of course, there were. After two or three minutes we were instructed to stop and open our eyes to see how many of our kind we had found. In small clusters were those who had found fellow cats, dogs, and horses, while I was immersed in a small herd of elephants. The parallel was not lost on us. We transmit unmistakable cues and signals about who we are and what we are seeking. Our group leaders encouraged us to think about our deepest held values and beliefs and move confidently in that direction. Whoever we were searching for was searching for us too.

Both of these exercises took on a more profound meaning when I came to faith in Christ. The whispered voices speaking words of love and devotion were reminiscent of the gentle, loving voice of God who had been wooing me since childhood. Many of us doubt that anyone loves us fully for who we are. We spend much of our lives hiding our real selves hoping no one discovers our true identity in fear that they would cease to love us. Not so with God. He sees us at our worst and offers us unconditional love. He tells us, *"Can a mother forget the baby at her breast and have no compassion on the child she has borne? Though she may forget, I will not forget you! See, I have engraved you on the palms of my hands"* (Isaiah 49:15, 16).

In Christ, I have realized the goal of those long-ago exercises: the certainty that I am dearly, deeply loved by the God who created me. He guided me to *"paths of righteousness" (Psalm 23:3)* where I found others who seek the kingdom of God. When I come across another Christian, I feel an immediate connection, a bond that's established by all the things we have in common. I'm at home with them. Along the way I've also learned some things about the noble elephant. These gentle, oversized creatures band together, have incredible strength, love and care for one another and carry heavy loads...attributes I've found in full measure in my Christian brothers and sisters.

Conversations at the Kitchen Table

- Are your friends a help or a hindrance to your faith? It's important to choose friends wisely because their influence is profound in ways that are varied and subtle. Many have unwittingly slipped into destructive lifestyles of drugs, alcohol, gambling, promiscuity and other vices by keeping close company with people who are careless about their lives. What advice do the following Scriptures contain?

  Proverbs 1:8-19
  Proverbs 13:20
  1 Corinthians 15:33

- There are several ways you can enlarge your circle of friends to include Christians who can support you in your faith walk. Look to your church's small group studies, women's ministries, adult ministries, fellowship events, support groups, volunteer opportunities and other ways to connect with those who will be glad to come alongside you and share your journey.

- Have you made Christ your closest companion? This is the start of your journey, your fork in the road, your point of departure from a life of frustration, anxiety, endless heartache, loneliness, lack and loss!

  What promise does Jesus make to assure us that we never walk alone? *Read Matthew 28:20.*

  Here I am! I stand at the door and knock. If anyone hears my voice and opens the door, I will come in and eat with him, and he with me (Revelation 3:20).

Lavish "Safari with Friends" Lunch

Today's lunch can serve a crowd so gather some of your fellow travelers together and share life safari stories! We make this ground turkey-veggie casserole using tri-colored pasta to give it additional color. Finish lunch with these sensational bar cookies...we make half of them with apricot preserves and the other half with raspberry!

Ground Turkey Pasta Bake
Extra virgin olive oil
1 pound ground turkey
2 cups fresh green beans, trimmed and cut into thirds
1 red pepper, diced
1 small onion, diced
1 clove garlic, minced
1 cup sliced mushrooms
2 cups pasta (rotini, penne, bow-tie)
1 (28-ounce) can tomato puree
1-1/2 teaspoons Italian seasoning
1/4 cup fresh chopped parsley
1 cup shredded mozzarella or Monterey Jack cheese

Preheat oven to 350 degrees. Prepare pasta per package directions. Brown ground turkey in 2 tablespoons of olive oil. Drain meat and spoon into large mixing bowl. Steam green beans for four minutes. Add to ground turkey. Sauté red peppers, onions, garlic and mushrooms in olive oil until vegetables are tender. Drain cooked pasta and combine with vegetables, ground turkey mixture, seasonings and one-half of the tomato pureé. Spoon into 13x9-inch casserole dish and cover with remaining pureé. Top with cheese and bake for 25-30 minutes.

Summer Fruit Bars
3 cups all purpose flour
2 cups rolled oats
1 teaspoon salt
1 teaspoon baking powder
1 cup packed brown sugar
3/4 cup softened butter
2 (8-ounce) packages cream cheese, softened
1 cup apricot preserves
1 cup raspberry preserves

Preheat oven to 400 degrees. In a large mixing bowl, combine flour, rolled oats, salt, baking powder and sugar. Add softened butter and cream cheese. With carefully washed hands, blend ingredients until thoroughly mixed. Reserve two cups of mixture. Press remaining mixture into a lightly greased 13x9-inch baking dish. Spread the apricot preserves on one half of the crust and the raspberry preserves on the other half. Crumble the reserved mixture on top of the preserves. Bake for 25-30 minutes or until lightly browned. Cool and as you cut into bars, you'll see the dividing line between the two preserves. Your friends and family will think you did twice the baking!

12

The American Dream...Who Could Want More?

When you have it all and it's not enough

*J*ulie writes...I certainly did. At 31, I had all of the trappings of worldly success. I was married to a handsome man with a promising career, had three adorable sons who were an absolute joy, a beautiful home filled with lovely possessions, and was surrounded by a supportive, loving group of family and friends. Still there was an emptiness gnawing at me that I couldn't define or relieve.

As a child and through my young adult years, I had knowledge about God, I had information about God, and I had facts about God. But I had no personal revelation of God. Looking back now, I realize that without that one-on-one experience, it's impossible for us to ever love Him and trust Him with our lives. Throughout those years, I was hot and cold toward God. I went through times of searching and thought I had found something on which to hang my faith. Then it would disappear, and I would be frozen cold again.

Now married and a mother, I was attending a church Bible study, still trying to obtain a greater connection to God. I noticed several women who seemed to have a special glow about them...an inner joy that radiated from them that made them stand out from others. I decided to ask one of them what it was that gave her such a graceful demeanor. She said I should seek the Lord...that's what had given her an inner peace. I was somewhat mystified by this. I wasn't sure what "seeking the Lord" meant or if it was any different than what I was already doing. Not long after, my husband mentioned that a couple of our friends had invited us to their home to learn about Jesus Christ. I was already learning about Jesus Christ in my Bible study, but was interested nonetheless, thinking perhaps they had some additional insight, a missing piece of the puzzle that had eluded me.

That night I learned what seeking the Lord really means. It's more than studying about Christ and memorizing facts about him. It's coming into a relationship with Him. It's experiencing the very presence of the Most High God. As we invite Him to join us when we sit quietly before Him, He will draw near and permeate our very beings. In unseen ways unknown to us, we are changed at the molecular level!

Our friends described how they had received assurance of God's love and forgiveness of their sins through the sacrifice of Christ. They explained how God continues to work in their lives through the power of the Holy Spirit, responding to their prayers, interceding for them, helping them make course corrections. They told us that if we decided to make the commitment to Christ that we should tell someone. I called them the next day to tell them I had decided in my heart to put Christ in charge of my life.

It's 25 years later and I no longer feel those pangs of emptiness inside. I thank God daily for His forgiveness and His continual love and guidance. *"I love those who love me, and those who seek me find me" (Proverbs 8:17).*

- What is your definition of the American dream? Has it brought you all that you thought it would?

- Do you "have it all" and still feel empty?

- Is it clear to you that no matter how many houses, possessions and toys you have, these things cannot feed your soul?

- Is your knowledge of God strictly based on "head knowledge" rather than "heart knowledge?" If so, will you commit to asking God everyday to reveal Himself to you?

Whoever comes to me I will never drive away (John 6:37).

But if from there you seek the Lord your God, you will find Him if you look for Him with all your heart and with all your soul (Deuteronomy 4:29).

Chances are there's a nearby friend or neighbor clutching the shards of a cracked American Dream. Invite her over to learn how you found your true inspiration in Christ!

South of the Border Chicken Stew
1 pound chicken breast strips
1 green, red, orange or yellow pepper (or a combination), diced
1 small onion, diced
1 can black beans
1 can diced Mexican-style tomatoes, undrained
1 (8-ounce) can diced green chilies
1-1/2 cups frozen organic corn
1 teaspoon each cumin and oregano
Salt and pepper
2 cups cooked brown rice
1/4 cup cilantro or fresh parsley

Cut chicken strips into bite-size pieces and sauté in olive oil with onions and peppers. Drain and rinse beans and add to skillet along with tomatoes, corn, chilies, and seasonings. Simmer until heated through. Combine rice and cilantro. Ladle stew into wide bowls and use an ice cream scoop to top each serving with cooked brown rice.

Three-Berry Crumble
Red, white and blue came to mind for Julie's "American Dream" message, and we decided on this three-berry crumble. Red, white and blue never looked better together than our raspberries and blueberries covered with a generous serving of vanilla ice cream or whipped cream!

Fruit Base
1-1/2 to 2 cups each: blueberries, raspberries, blackberries
1/2 cup sugar
1 teaspoon lemon zest
2 teaspoons lemon juice
1 teaspoon cornstarch

Topping
1 cup brown sugar
1 cup old fashioned oats
1/2 cup flour
1 teaspoon cinnamon
1/2 cup butter, cut in pieces

Preheat oven to 375 degrees. Butter a two-quart baking dish. Combine berries, sugar and lemon zest in a mixing bowl. Stir together lemon juice and cornstarch till smooth. Toss gently with berries and spoon into baking dish. For topping, combine oats, brown sugar, flour, cinnamon and butter in a bowl. Sprinkle over berries and bake in center rack for 50-60 minutes. If topping browns too quickly, cover with foil for the last 15 minutes. Serve warm with ice cream or whipped cream.

13

Practicing His Presence
Practice makes perfect…when we imitate Christ

Many Christians express a desire to have a closer relationship with God but don't know how to get started. We can begin each day by practicing His presence. We can go about our lives as if He cared, as if He loved us, as if He longed to communicate with us, as if He could untangle and restore the broken pieces of our lives that now lie mangled beyond our ability to repair. Because He does, He can and He will! Acting "as if" will bear out the truth of this in our lives.

Then we seek Him out in the pages of Scripture where He reveals His heart, telling us He's near. His tenderness and devotion are fully displayed in this love song He sings to us:

> *"The Lord your God is with you,*
> *He is mighty to save.*
> *He will take great delight in you,*
> *He will quiet you with his love,*
> *He will rejoice over you with singing."*
> *(Zephaniah 3:17)*

Then we invite Him in to the hidden places in our lives, the areas where we've shut the door and stand guard lest anyone try to enter. Maybe it involves our finances, a habit we don't want to break or a relationship we don't want to give up. We'll experience an uneasy restlessness in our spirits until we give Him permission to take charge. He won't override our will… we are not puppets He wants to control, but agents of free will. How about if we let Him pilot our wayward Titanics before they hit that iceberg! *"Remain in me and I will remain in you. No branch can bear fruit by itself; it must remain in the vine. Neither can you bear fruit unless you remain in me" (John 15:4).*

Then we pray on a daily basis and talk to Him as we would our best friend because no one else will ever hold us closer. We take Him at His word and trust in the promise that He will never leave or forsake us. *"And surely I am with you always, to the very end of the age."*

(Matthew 28:20). We act as if that's true…because it is! From this point on it's all about trust. As children of God, we need to know our way around our Father's house. This "trust alphabet" will take us on a tour:

Trust and **a**bide – *He who dwells in the shelter of the Most High will rest in the shadow of the Almighty (Psalm 91:1).*

Trust and **b**elieve – *…whatever you ask for in prayer, believe that you have received it, and it will be yours (Mark 11:24).*

Trust and **c**onfess – *That if you confess with your mouth, "Jesus is Lord," and believe in your heart that God raised him from the dead, you will be saved (Romans 10:9).*

Trust and **d**oubt not – *My heart trusts in Him, and I am helped (Psalm 28:7).*

Trust and **e**ndure – *Endure hardship as discipline; God is treating you as sons. For what son is not disciplined by his father? (Hebrews 12:7).*

Trust and **f**ear not – *Do not be afraid, little flock, for your Father has been pleased to give you the kingdom (Luke 12:32).*

Trust and **g**ive thanks – *Give thanks to the Lord, for He is good (Psalm 136:1).*

Trust and **h**ope – *…we wait for the blessed hope-the glorious appearing of our great God and Savior, Jesus Christ (Titus 2:13).*

Trust and **i**mitate – *Be imitators of God, therefore, as dearly loved children and live a life of love, just as Christ loved us (Ephesians 5:1).*

Trust and **j**oyful remain – *…the joy of the Lord is your strength (Nehemiah 8:10).*

Trust and **k**eep faith – *Now faith is the substance of things hoped for, the evidence of things not seen (Hebrews 11:1 KJV).*

Trust and **l**ove – *Love is patient, love is kind… it keeps no record of wrongs. It always protects, always trusts, always hopes, always perseveres. Love never fails (1 Corinthians 13:4-8).*

Trust and **m**otivate – *Each helps the other and says to his brother, "Be strong!" (Isaiah 41:6).*

Trust and **n**ourish – *The lips of the righteous nourish many… (Proverbs 10:21).*

Trust and **o**bey – *Blessed rather are those who hear the word of God and obey it (Luke 11:28.)*

Trust and **p**ray – *Watch and pray so that you will not fall into temptation (Matthew 26:41).*

Trust and **q**uit complaining - *Do everything without complaining or arguing, so that you may become blameless and pure, children of God, without fault in a crooked and depraved generation… (Philippians 2:14).*

Trust and **r**ejoice – *…my soul rejoices in my God. For he has clothed me with garments of salvation and arrayed me in a robe of righteousness (Isaiah 61:10).*

Trust and **s**ing – *I will sing to the Lord, for He has been good to me (Psalm 13:6).*

Trust and **t**each – *Preach the Word; be prepared in season and out of season (2 Timothy 4:2).*

Trust and **u**nderstand – *Therefore do not be foolish, but understand what the Lord's will is (Ephesians 5:17).*

Trust and **v**alue your pearls - *…do not throw your pearls to pigs (Matthew 7:6).*

Trust and **w**ait – *…wait for his Son from heaven, whom He raised from the dead: Jesus who rescues us from the coming wrath (1 Thessalonians 1:10).*

Corinthians 13:5).

Trust and y̲ield – …yield yourselves unto God, as those that are alive from the dead, and your members as instruments of righteousness unto God (Romans 6:13 KJV).

Trust and z̲ealously pursue God – *…he was zealous for the honor of his God (Numbers 25:13).*

Let's continue to seek the hope, the promise, the truth, grace, beauty and divine wisdom that unfold in the pages of Scripture. Our Heavenly Father eagerly and joyfully awaits us!

- Reread *Zephaniah 3:17*. Have you experienced the love of God in this way – intimate, personal and lovingly tender? We won't necessarily experience this every day, but it's important to have a revelation of God's love to withstand the slings and arrows of life. Memorize this verse and bring it to mind when you feel sad, distressed, alone or need strength to go out and slay dragons!

- If God seems distant and remote, ask Him to give you a personal revelation of His love for you as you sit quietly in His presence. Then give it some time. What are you to think about while waiting? Paul suggests some thought-starters in *Philippians 4:8*. If you don't sense anything the first few times, don't quit! Show up faithfully, be consistent! One day you'll encounter the unmistakable presence of Almighty God!

- Remember that God speaks to us through Scripture as well as through circumstances and other people. Any number of family members, friends or even strangers can come alongside us in our times of crisis and "be Jesus" to us…and we can do this for others as well. These are ways God demonstrates His love for us.

- Are there areas of your life that you are withholding from God? Why not trust Him with one of those areas right now? As hard as it may be to relinquish control, He will prove faithful and cause us to live without regret.

- Where do you need work on the "trust alphabet?" Talk to God about it. Where we are weak, He is strong!

"My grace is sufficient for you, for my power is made perfect in weakness" (2 Corinthians 12:9).

Lavish "Rehearsal" Lunch

Let's practice God's presence as we prepare lunch today. The more we bring Him to mind, the more we'll be blessed by His presence! Serve today's treat on a lacy paper cut-out on a glass plate!

Crabmeat~Mushroom Bake
1 (6-8 ounce) package frozen crabmeat, thawed
5 or 6 strips cooked bacon
1/2 cup chopped celery
1/2 cup minced onion
1 cup sliced fresh mushrooms
1 clove finely chopped garlic
2 tablespoons flour
1/2 teaspoon salt
Dash pepper
1/2 cup milk
1/2 cup dry white wine
1 cup shredded Monterey Jack cheese
2 cups cooked brown rice
1/2 cup grated Parmesan cheese

Preheat oven to 350 degrees. Drain and chop crabmeat. In a large skillet, sauté celery, mushrooms, onion and garlic until tender. Blend in flour, salt and pepper. Slowly add milk and cook over low heat, stirring constantly, until thickened and smooth. Stir in wine. Add crab, crumbled bacon and cheese to sauce. Mix with cooked rice. Turn into 13x9-inch pan. Sprinkle with Parmesan cheese and bake 25-30 minutes.

Angel Tea Party Treats
Filling
1 (8-ounce) package cream cheese, softened
1 cup sweetened condensed milk
1/3 cup lemon juice
1 teaspoon vanilla

Pastry
1 cup butter, softened
1-1/2 cups all purpose flour
1/2 cup powdered sugar
1 tablespoon cornstarch

Toppings
2 tablespoons cherry or raspberry jam
2 tablespoons cocoa

Coconut
Ground walnuts
Semi-sweet chocolate shavings

Preheat oven to 325 degrees. Beat cream cheese until smooth. Gradually beat in condensed milk, lemon juice and vanilla. Cover and refrigerate eight hours or overnight. To make pastry, beat flour, butter, powdered sugar and cornstarch until smooth. Roll into one-inch balls and press into mini-muffin tins. Prick with a fork and bake for 15 minutes or until lightly golden. Let tarts rest for a few minutes before removing from pan. Pastry will bake up to the top of tart cups, so make indentations in each tart with the back of a spoon to hold the filling.

Meanwhile, remove cream cheese filling from refrigerator and separate into three bowls. First bowl of filling has no additions. To the second bowl, mix in cherry or raspberry jam; to the third bowl, mix in cocoa. Divide the three fillings evenly among the pastry tarts. Top the plain cream cheese filled tarts with ground walnuts and coconuts; top cherry filled tarts with a fresh or frozen raspberry; top chocolate filled tarts with a mound of grated semi-sweet chocolate.

14

The Jewel of Contentment
Chasing after things leaves us broke, exhausted and unfulfilled

We are a restless people in a state of constant craving. We are never satisfied, even when we have achieved and possess far beyond what we could have imagined a few years or a decade ago. It's not our nature to be content. We are continually on the hunt for the next wave, the next big thing. We strategize, scheme and map out another game plan to get whatever the next "must have" is and to get there ahead of the next guy.

This natural drive to achieve and acquire never brings us lasting contentment. The very thing that would satisfy our craving, however, is not something we are seeking: the peace and contentment found only in God. Solomon, the richest and wisest of Israel's kings, pursued life's pleasures with a vengeance. He set out to have it all and acquired wives, harems, houses, gardens, parks, vineyards, herds, flocks, silver and gold, treasures of kings and provinces and every desirable commodity. In the book of Ecclesiastes, he writes of his pleasure-seeking pastimes and the meaninglessness of it all that is the final result:

"I denied myself nothing my eyes desired; I refused my heart no pleasure. My heart took delight in all my work, and this was the reward for all my labor. Yet when I surveyed all that my hands had done and what I had toiled to achieve, everything was meaningless, a chasing after the wind; nothing was gained under the sun" (Ecclesiastes 2:10-11).

Bible stories and first-hand accounts such as this one from Solomon are there to benefit us so we don't fall into the same traps. It's just too silly for all of us to make the same mistakes! Yet we see the same chasing after things in today's culture where a popular expression is: "He who dies with the most toys wins." Jesus cautions against such a materialistic philosophy in *Luke 12:15, "Watch out! Be on your guard against all kinds of greed; a man's life does not consist in the abundance of his possessions."*

An alternative view is offered in *1 Timothy 6:6-10: "But godliness with contentment is great gain. For we brought nothing into the world, and we can take nothing out of it. But if we have food and clothing, we will be content with that. People who want to get rich fall into temptation and a trap and into many foolish and harmful desires that plunge men into ruin and destruction. For the love of money is a root of all kinds of evil. Some people, eager for money, have wandered from the faith and pierced themselves with many griefs."* All of our striving after things is nothing more than a snare of the enemy. If he can keep us busy and focused on material things, we'll have little or no room for God.

The first of the Ten Commandments is explicit: *"'I am the Lord your God...you shall have no other gods before me'" (Exodus 20:2, 3)*. God clearly wants to be first in our lives. Other gods before Him can include money, possessions, power, a relationship, career, hobby or anything that we put ahead of Him. As long as any of these things occupy first place in our lives, our contentment will be short-lived. Only in God do we find the fulfillment our souls search after. In difficult days and times of trial, our possessions will be of no solace. It's the contentment and peace of God that will be our saving grace.

<u>Conversations at the Kitchen Table</u>

- What does contentment mean to you?

- What does Solomon teach us about having everything under the sun?

- Have possessions, a career or an outside interest overtaken your life? What steps can you take to achieve better balance?

- Do the possessions you've had for a long time still thrill you years later? Have you ever opened a credit card bill and couldn't recall any of the items you had charged? Have you ever gone through a closet or drawer and discovered a purchase made years ago with the tags still attached? What about the "must-have-at-any cost" items now tagged for a garage sale? These are clues that what we think we have to have doesn't satisfy or fulfill us in the long run.

- God desires for us to seek Him above all things. *"Love the Lord your God with all your heart and with all your soul and with all your strength" (Deuteronomy 6:5).* Ask God to place this desire in your heart.

- Setting aside our own agendas to follow after God will ultimately bring us to the place of greatest fulfillment.

  "Delight yourself in the Lord and He will give you the desires of your heart" (Psalm 37:4)

  "Better is one day in your courts than a thousand elsewhere; I would rather be a doorkeeper in the house of my God than dwell in the tents of the wicked. For the Lord God is a sun and shield; the Lord bestows favor and honor; no good thing does He withhold from those whose walk is blameless. O Lord Almighty, blessed is the man who trusts in you" (Psalm 84:10-12).

Lavish "Satisfy Me" Lunch

In our moments of discontent, more than likely our focus has been on something negative. Let's refocus on the blessings that continually flow toward us as children of God and *"...declare the praises of Him who called you out of darkness into His wonderful light" (1Peter 2:9)*. Today's lunch can't help but restore a joyful mood!

Garden Crustada
1 cup cottage cheese
1 cup plain yogurt
1/4 cup flour
1/4 teaspoon baking powder
1/2 teaspoon baking soda
2 beaten eggs
1/2 cup plus 2 tablespoons Parmesan cheese, divided
2 medium tomatoes, thinly sliced
3/4 cup sliced mushrooms
1-1/2 cups broccoli florets
2 tablespoons fresh, chopped parsley

Preheat oven to 350 degrees. Spray an 11x7-inch casserole dish with nonstick cooking spray. In a food processor or blender place cottage cheese, yogurt, flour, baking powder, baking soda, pepper, beaten eggs and 1/3 cup Parmesan cheese. Process or blend until smooth. Arrange half the tomatoes on the bottom of the prepared dish. Add mushrooms layering on top and around tomatoes. Place broccoli over tomatoes and mushrooms. Pour half the cheese mixture on top of broccoli. Arrange remaining tomatoes on top of mixture. Pour remaining cheese mixture on top. Sprinkle with remaining Parmesan cheese and parsley. Bake for 35 to 40 minutes or until top is lightly golden. Remove from oven and let stand 10 minutes before serving.

Pumpkin-Chocolate Chip Cookies
1 cup pumpkin
3/4 cup sugar
1/3 cup oil
1 egg
2 cups flour
2 teaspoons baking powder
1/2 teaspoon cinnamon
1/2 teaspoon salt
1 cup chocolate chips
1 cup walnuts, chopped
1 teaspoon vanilla
1 teaspoon baking soda

Preheat oven to 375 degrees. In large bowl, mix pumpkin, sugar, oil and egg. In second bowl, mix the flour, baking powder, cinnamon and salt. Add dry ingredients to the pumpkin mixture. Add chocolate chips, nuts, vanilla and baking soda. Drop by teaspoonfuls onto lightly greased cookie sheets and bake for 8-10 minutes.

15

Suiting Up For Battle: Don't Forget Your Helmet
An up-close look at our weapons of warfare

We'd like you to sit down with a nice cup of herbal tea to soothe you while we deliver some bad news: as new Christians enlist in God's army, they get drafted for war. Whether or not we realize it, we're the newest recruits in an epic battle between the Kingdom of God and His longtime foe, the enemy of our souls. He has many names…Satan, Lucifer, the serpent, the evil one, the accuser, the destroyer, the enemy of our souls, father of lies. While the names and disguises vary, his game never does: to drag as many unsuspecting souls to hell as he can. In his case, misery surely loves company. He plays for keeps and has our names on his hit list.

Scripture tells us, *"Your enemy the devil prowls around like a roaring lion looking for someone to devour" (1 Peter 5:8).* His mission is *"to steal and kill and destroy…" John 10:10).* He's been around a long time, has certain powers, studies us closely and knows our every weakness. Taking this warning lightly or not at all will result in the infliction of heavy casualties.

Now for the good news! Satan has already been vanquished by the sacrifice Christ made at Calvary. He's just not in permanent lock-up yet. His day is coming though, and until then he's feverishly intent on increasing the population for his chamber of horrors.

That doesn't include us, though. Because we belong to Christ, Satan can't destroy us. But he can beat us up and waylay us at every turn. His aim is to do everything in his power to neutralize our testimony and keep us from being effective in the Kingdom. Scripture unmasks his nefarious ways and methods so we don't have to be conned by his tricks. *"Submit your-selves, then, to God. Resist the devil, and he will flee from you" (James 4:7).* Whatever has come against us, we want to find the promise in Scripture that addresses our need and stand upon His word. God's word is truth and whatever stands opposed to it ultimately has to yield. *"No weapon forged against you will prevail" (Isaiah 54:17).* Feel like a little comfort food at this point? Let's stop here for a moment and sample today's treat: a still warm Fruit-Yogurt Brûlée!

The Apostle Paul lays out the battle plan in *Ephesians 6:10-13: "Finally, be strong in the Lord and in his mighty power. Put on the full armor of God so that you can take your stand against the devil's schemes. For our struggle is not against flesh and blood, but against the rulers, against the authorities, against the powers of this dark world and against the spiritual forces of evil in the heavenly realms. Therefore put on the full armor of God, so that when the day of evil comes, you may be able to stand your ground, and after you have done everything, to stand."*

Our weapons of warfare are listed in *Ephesians 6:14-18: "Stand firm then, with the belt of truth buckled around your waist, with the breastplate of righteousness in place, and with your feet fitted with the readiness that comes from the gospel of peace. In addition to all this, take up the shield of faith, with which you can extinguish all the flaming arrows of the evil one. Take the helmet of salvation and the sword of the Spirit, which is the word of God. And pray in the spirit on all occasions..."*

A wonderful morning exercise includes mentally picturing ourselves putting on our battle dress. A variety of unexpected problems and difficulties can loom on the horizon, but if we begin our day mentally and spiritually prepared, we'll be ready to look them full in the face and not flinch. Let's take a look at each one of our weapons:

Belt of truth. Jesus tells us, *"If you hold to my teachings, you are really my disciples. Then you will know the truth, and the truth will set you free" (John 8:31, 32)*. Notice the word "if." Holding to His teachings means not just in the first blush of an emotional highpoint, but faithfully, consistently adhering to them on a day-by-day basis even when the road is dry and dusty. *"I am the way and the truth and the life" (John 14:6)*.

Breastplate of righteousness. Through Christ, our sins are covered, and we are cloaked in His righteousness. No enemy attack will penetrate this breastplate barrier or prevent Christ from presenting us *"without fault and with great joy" (Jude 24)* to God the Father.

Shoes of peace. Is it really possible to possess a peace that holds us steady even though the bottom may have dropped out from under us? Jesus is the Prince of Peace *(Isaiah 9:6)* and peace is our heritage regardless of whatever nightmare situation we may be facing. *"You will keep in perfect peace him whose mind is steadfast, because he trusts in you" (Isaiah 26:3)*.

Shield of faith. Faith is believing the word of God no matter what the circumstances look like. It is having full and unwavering confidence in our Father's word. Faith will serve as a covering to ward off the enemy's fiery darts. *"He will cover you with his feathers, and under his wings you will find refuge; his faithfulness will be your shield and rampart" (Psalm 91:4)*.

Helmet of salvation. Jesus' shed blood secured our salvation. Once we come into His sheepfold, nothing and no one can take that away from us. *"I give them eternal life, and they shall never perish; no one can snatch them out of my hand"(John 10:28)*. No matter what happens to us in this lifetime, our eternal destiny with God and His Christ is secured.

Sword of the spirit. *"For the word of God is living and active...sharper than any double-edged sword" (Hebrews 4:12)*. Satan fled when Jesus rebuffed his lures with the Word in *Matthew 4:1-11*. Whether we are faced with temptation, hit by calamity, overwhelmed by

98

insurmountable obstacles, followers of Christ are to do as He did and speak the Word to our impossible situations. *"I tell you the truth, if you have faith as small as a mustard seed, you can say to this mountain, 'Move from here to there' and it will move. Nothing will be impossible for you" (Matthew 17:20).*

Battle armor…don't leave home without it!

Conversations at the Kitchen Table

- Do you recognize that as a Christian you are in a spiritual battle?

- Are you using your weapons of warfare?

- Have you lost any battles because your armor was nowhere in sight?

- Can you identify a victory when you had your weapons of warfare ready?

- Read the story of David and Goliath (*1 Samuel 17*) to get a picture of a young shepherd who used his faith to face a giant enemy warrior and defeat him. With God at our side, a battle ax is no match for a slingshot!

  "All my enemies will be ashamed and dismayed; they will turn back in sudden disgrace" (Psalm 6:10).

  "The Lord is my light and my salvation – whom shall I fear? The Lord is the stronghold of my life – of whom shall I be afraid? When evil men advance against me to devour my flesh, when my enemies and my foes attack me, they will stumble and fall. Though an army besiege me, my heart will not fear; though war break out against me, even then will I be confident" (Psalm 27:1-3).

- Our own resources will not take us very far. Only with the never-ending supply of God's inexhaustible power can we go the distance. Read and reflect on *Psalm 18*.

  "For the eyes of the Lord range throughout the earth to strengthen those whose hearts are fully committed to him" (2 Chronicles 16:9).

Lavish "Warriors" Lunch

If there are new Christians in your midst, this is a great company dish to serve on your way to getting to know them better! Plus it's another way to include some salmon in your diet.

Salmon Torta with Creamy Horseradish Sauce
1/2 cup couscous
1 (10-ounce) package frozen spinach (thaw and squeeze dry)
1 beaten egg
1/4 cup finely chopped onion
2 celery stalks, chopped
1 cup sliced mushrooms
1/2 cup milk
1/2 cup Monterey Jack cheddar cheese
14 ounces of fresh red salmon or one can drained, flaked salmon
2 eggs
2 tablespoons fresh parsley
Creamy horseradish sauce (recipe below)

Heat oven to 350 degrees and spray a 10-inch pie plate with non-stick spray. Prepare couscous and combine with spinach and egg. Put mixture into lightly greased pie plate. Sauté onions, celery and mushrooms in olive oil until tender. Place in a mixing bowl and add milk, cheese, salmon, lightly beaten eggs and chopped parsley. Press mixture into bottom and up sides of pie plate, spooning evenly over couscous crust. Bake 40-45 minutes or until heated through. Let rest 10 minutes before cutting. Serve with creamy horseradish sauce: 1 cup sour cream or light mayonnaise, and 2-3 tablespoons horseradish.

Fruit-Yogurt Brûlée
2 cups plain yogurt, drained
2 cups fresh fruit of your choice (peaches, bananas or berries work great)
1/4 cup brown sugar

Drain yogurt in cheesecloth or a coffee filter placed in a strainer set in a small bowl in the refrigerator for several hours or overnight to remove liquid. Preheat broiler. Divide fruit in six 4-ounce ramekin cups. Spoon two heaping tablespoons of yogurt over fruit and sprinkle with two teaspoons brown sugar. Place ramekins in jelly roll pan and broil 2-3 minutes until sugar melts/bubbles.

16

Get Aligned To Message Pillars
A corporate-speak memo that delivers a powerful message

*A*rlene writes…The phrase "get aligned to message pillars" was part of a coaching memo to the communications staff of my former company. The memo provided tips on achieving consistency in communications tone and appearance. The phrase made me think of a Dilbert cartoon having all the earmarks of "corporate-speak." I've grown fond of it nonetheless. I have no clue what the particular message pillar was they were asking people to align with…but it's perfect for the message I want to convey here.

Having just watched the DVD set of the *Lord of the Rings* trilogy, I was intrigued at the manner in which the fellowship team kept moving forward against the massive assault of the evil forces arrayed against them. Quite simply, they aligned to a "message pillar." Hope was the theme that governed this inspired story. No matter how bleak, gloomy, futile, beaten, battered and defeated their situation sometimes appeared, they aligned to the message pillar of hope. They held fast to the doctrine that every setback was temporary, that every losing battle was not the end of the war, but that in every step backward would come the momentum needed to advance two steps forward, that *"…no weapon forged against you will prevail…" (Isaiah 54:17)*. They aligned to the message pillar of hope. And evil was finally vanquished.

We too will face days or seasons of darkness when it seems that the forces of hell itself have come against us. And in these underground tunnels where no light penetrates, we can make our way by aligning to our message pillars.

- Pillars of Hope… *"Those who hope in the Lord will renew their strength. They will soar on wings like eagles; they will run and not grow weary, they will walk and not be faint" (Isaiah 40:31).*

- Pillars of Faith… *"He who began a good work in you will carry it on to completion until the day of Christ Jesus" (Philippians 1:6).*

- Pillars of Trust… *"Even though I walk through the valley of the shadow of death, I will fear no evil, for you are with me" (Psalm 23:4).*

Message pillars…there are hundreds of them in Scripture. Search them out. Then align to your message pillars. *"For great is his love toward us, and the faithfulness of the Lord endures forever" (Psalm 117:2).*

Conversations at the Kitchen Table

- Have you identified several message pillars you can align with in times of fear, discouragement or heartache?

- If not, now might be a good time to select a number of Scriptures that speak hope to your heart and memorize them!

- Find some favorite Scriptures and commit them to memory. You'll be amazed at how meditating on them will help you through difficult, stressful or painful situations. They will be a source of comfort and peace that covers you when your Bible is miles away! Here are some memory suggestions to get you started:

Proverbs 3:5, 6
Ephesians 3:16-20
Psalm 23
Psalm 91
Romans 8:28
Philippians 4:6, 7

Lavish "Hope in our Hearts" Lunch

This is an angel of a dish! The coconut bars are pretty awesome too.

Baked Pasta Angeliera
8 ounces whole wheat spaghetti pasta
1 tablespoon olive oil
1 cup chopped onions
2 cloves garlic, finely chopped
1/4 cup chopped parsley
1 tablespoon lemon juice
1 teaspoon oregano
1 teaspoon basil
1/2 cup ricotta cheese
1 egg white
1/2 cup Parmesan cheese
2 cups veggie medley: chopped broccoli, cauliflower, zucchini, mushrooms
1 cup Alfredo sauce, divided
1/4 cup mozzarella cheese

Preheat oven to 375 degrees. Cover bottom of an 8-inch springform pan with aluminum foil allowing several inches of foil to overlap pan bottom. Grease and flour foil. Close pan and press foil up against outside of pan to eliminate leaks. Cook pasta and drain. Saute onions and garlic. Add to pasta along with parsley, lemon juice, oregano and basil. In a small bowl combine ricotta, egg white, 2 tablespoons of Parmesan. Add to the pasta and toss well. Turn half the pasta-cheese mixture into prepared pan and press lightly over bottom. Arrange veggies on top, spoon 1/2 cup Alfredo sauce over veggies and sprinkle with half the mozzarella cheese. Top with remaining pasta-cheese. Top with remaining sauce, mozzarella cheese and remaining Parmesan. Cover with foil and bake 40 minutes. Cool for 10 minutes and cut into wedges.

Coconut-Date Bars
1/2 cup butter
3/4 cup brown sugar
1 egg
1 teaspoon vanilla
2/3 cup flour
1 teaspoon salt
1/2 teaspoon baking powder
1 cup rolled oats
1 cup flaked coconut
1 cup fresh dates, chopped
1/2 cup nuts, chopped

Preheat oven to 350 degrees. Cream together butter and brown sugar until light and fluffy. Blend in egg and vanilla. Combine flour, salt and baking powder and add to creamed mixture. Stir in oats, coconut, dates and nuts. Spread into greased 9-inch square pan. Bake 30 minutes. Cool and cut into bars.

17

Under Construction: Pardon Our Dust

*The renovating process begins at salvation and continues
until Christ calls us home*

Becoming Christ-like is a process not unlike that of renovating one's house. Huge portions of the house are left intact while one room at a time undergoes reconstruction. Unlike the house project, however, our spiritual houses will never be finished this side of eternity. The important thing is that it gets started.

In another session, we discussed that the whole process begins when the Holy Spirit enlightens us to our sinful nature and floods our hearts with faith in Jesus. From that point on, the Holy Spirit's job is to guide us into greater truth. He will begin work on one area after another until our spiritual houses become more and more like the Savior we follow.

He doesn't do it all in one fell swoop, thank God! He spotlights one at a time the areas in our lives that need to be changed. Then He enlists our cooperation in bringing about our transformation. If we saw the entire defective picture at one sitting, it would no doubt sink our hopes of ever getting such a massive undertaking completed at all.

Some areas may be relatively painless for us to yield to the Holy Spirit. As soon as we're made aware of sinful practices or attitudes that displease God, we find it easy to cast them aside. In other instances, however, the roots of a particular sin run deep and may be something we don't think we can give up. The renovating effort can seem like a slow ascension through layers of mud and filth from some deep subterranean cave out of which we climb still caked with the slime of the pit. The process is humbling and sometimes difficult to face. It helps to know that God is not surprised. He already knows our weaknesses and vulnerabilities.

The Holy Spirit's purpose in shining light on our dark areas is for us to see them. We can speed up or slow down our progress by acknowledging our condition or avoiding and refusing to deal with it. It pays to remember, however, that the Holy Spirit will get the job done. Any portion of a house that won't give under the master builder's tools will ultimately be subjected to a more forceful blast by dynamite or a wrecking ball. "'*My son, do not make light of the*

Lord's discipline, and do not lose heart when he rebukes you, because the Lord disciplines those he loves, and he punishes everyone he accepts as a son'"(Hebrews 12:5, 6).

God's aim is to burn out the impurities and bring us forth as pure gold, *"...so that you may be able to discern what is best and may be pure and blameless until the day of Christ, filled with the fruit of righteousness that comes through Jesus Christ-to the glory and praise of God"* (Philippians 1:10 ,11). To be pure and blameless is too lofty a vision for any of us to achieve on our own. A transformation of this magnitude is a painstaking process that is accomplished solely through the work of the Holy Spirit. Our part is simply to yield to the power at work in us, *"being confident of this, that he who began a good work in you is able to bring it to the day of completion..."* (Philippians 1:6).

Conversations at the Kitchen Table

- In what ways do you feel the Holy Spirit at work in your life?

- Can you identify any areas He wants to renovate that you are resisting?

- If so, have you prayed and asked His help in breaking the power of whatever has you captive?

- Have you enlisted an accountability partner who can pray for you and help you to stay on track with any areas of struggle?

- The apostle Paul tells the church at Philippi *"continue to work out your salvation with fear and trembling, for it is God who works in you to will and to act according to his good purpose"(Philippians 2:12, 13).* Don't let the words "fear and trembling" scare you. It simply means pursue God and build your faith with purpose and intention. Let's not be lax, lazy, sloppy and careless with so great a gift as salvation! *"Do your best to present yourself to God as one approved, a workman who does not need to be ashamed and who correctly handles the word of truth" (2 Timothy 2:15).*

- Read *Hebrews 12:7-8*. Why should we endure hardship?

- What are some things we can do to build up our faith? Read *Joshua 1:8*

Lavish "Remodel" Lunch

Personal remodeling projects take energy, encouragement and occasional rewards! Our main dish provides the first, and these scrumptious sweet potato bars deliver on the last two!

Chicken-Mushroom-Artichoke Casserole
5 tablespoons butter, divided
1 pound chicken breast strips, cut into bite-size pieces
2 cups fresh sliced mushrooms
1/2 cup onions
2 tablespoons flour
Salt and pepper to taste
1 cup organic chicken broth
1/4 cup milk
1 teaspoon lemon juice
1 teaspoon ground nutmeg
1 (14-ounce) can artichoke hearts, well drained
1/2 cup shredded Monterey Jack cheese
3/4 cup soft bread crumbs

Preheat oven to 350 degrees. In a medium skillet, melt 4 tablespoons butter. Add mushrooms and onions and sauté until vegetables are tender. Add chicken and brown on both sides. Remove from pan and set aside. In same pan, add remaining tablespoon of butter, flour, salt and pepper; cook one minute, stirring constantly. Gradually add broth, milk, lemon juice and nutmeg. Cook and continue stirring until thickened and bubbly. Stir back in chicken, mushrooms, and onions and add artichokes and shredded cheese. Turn into lightly greased one-quart casserole. Combine breadcrumbs and another tablespoon of melted butter. Sprinkle on top of casserole. Bake 30 to 35 minutes until bubbly hot.

Sweet Potato Bars
Crust
1/2 cup butter
3/4 cup brown sugar
1 cup all purpose flour

Filling
1/4 cup butter
3/4 cup brown sugar
1-1/2 cups all purpose flour
1/2 cup sweetened condensed milk
1 teaspoon cinnamon
1/2 teaspoon nutmeg
1/4 teaspoon salt
1 egg

2 medium sweet potatoes, baked and mashed

<u>Topping</u>
1 (8 ounce) package cream cheese, room temperature
1 teaspoon vanilla
5-6 drops Stevia (a natural, non-caloric, sweet-tasting alternative to sugar)

Preheat oven to 350 degrees. Grease and flour 13x9-inch baking pan. Beat 1/2 cup butter and 3/4 cup brown sugar in bowl until fluffy. Beat in 1 cup flour until combined. Press mixture in pan and bake 10-12 minutes.

Beat 1/4 cup butter and 3/4 cup brown sugar in bowl until fluffy. Add flour, condensed milk, seasonings, egg and sweet potatoes and mix until combined. Spoon evenly over baked crust. Bake 30-35 minutes until set. Mix topping ingredients until smooth and spread over cooled cake.

18

The Prodigal Son

The story of mankind lost and the Father who awaits our return

The prodigal son is the story of mankind lost. It is the age-old story of sin and its tantalizing lures that disguise the ruin at its end. It also paints a beautiful portrait of our loving heavenly Father patiently waiting the day when we'll turn our hearts toward home, where He is waiting to welcome us with open arms.

In *Luke 15:11-32*, Jesus tells the story of the prodigal son who asked his father for his inheritance and left home for far off lands. There he squandered his treasure on wild living. When the money was gone, so were his friends. A famine came and soon the son found himself slopping pigs with no place to live and nothing to eat. As pigs were considered unclean in his culture, his descent into living alongside them was the ultimate degradation.

Sin always holds out the promise of life beyond our imaginations and the fulfillment of our every dream, but leaves us empty, lost and full of despair. In his misery, it dawned on the prodigal that the servants in his father's house were far better off. At once he arose, determined to go home and tell his father that he had come to a ruinous end and was willing to be a servant in his household if he would only take him back.

His father, faithful and ever watchful, saw him coming from a long way off and ran to meet him with a new coat and a ring for his finger. He called to the servants to prepare the fatted calf for a feast because this son who was lost had now come home. In *Luke 15:7*, Jesus declares *"…there will be more rejoicing in heaven over one sinner who repents than over ninety-nine righteous persons who do not need to repent."* Our Heavenly Father, long-suffering and slow to anger, rejoices when he sees us rising from the pigsty in the foreign land where we have settled and begin to make our way back to him.

We, like many Christian prodigals, have wandered off, squandered time and treasure and taken up residence in a land not ours. When we realize the ultimate futility of living a life without God and call upon Him, He lovingly restores our status as "King's kids."

There is no sin so dark, so deep, so wretched, and so habitual that He will not forgive; no transgression he will not cover with the blood of His son when we confess it, repent and turn from it. God says in *Isaiah 1:18, "Though your sins are like scarlet, they shall be as white as snow; though they are red as crimson, they shall be like wool."*

The prodigal son woke up and witnessed firsthand that the wages of sin are indeed death. After failing in his pitiful attempt to "run his own railroad," he came to his senses and understood the "no-brainer" decision that lay before him: leave the pig farm and return home to a life of abundance, restored relationship, love everlasting and blessings that last not for a season but for all eternity.

Conversations at the Kitchen Table

- Where do you see yourself in the story of the prodigal?

- Can you pinpoint a particular God-moment where he opened your eyes to your situation?

- How has He helped you to leave the foreign land and return home?

- If you feel like you're still in a foreign land and God is far away, read the following passage in Lamentations, and ask God to guide you out of exile and lead you home!

"I remember my afflictions and my wandering, the bitterness and the gall. I well remember them, and my soul is downcast within me. Yet this I call to mind and therefore I have hope: Because of the Lord's great love we are not consumed, for his compassions never fail. They are new every morning; great is your faithfulness. I say to myself, "The Lord is my portion; therefore I will wait for him. The Lord is good to those whose hope is in him, to the one who seeks him; it is good to wait quietly for the salvation of the Lord" (Lamentations 3:19-26).

- God is a God of many chances. Even though we disappoint Him thousands of times, He still is willing to grant compassion and mercy to those who belong to Him.

"Yet he was merciful; he forgave their iniquities and did not destroy them. Time after time he restrained his anger and did not stir up his full wrath. He remembered that they were but flesh, a passing breeze that does not return" (Psalm 78:38-39).

Lavish "Welcome Home" Lunch

We thought this Beef Burgundy dish would serve as a stand-in for the fatted calf that's referenced in today's session. Perhaps the welcome home celebration would have included a dessert something along the lines of this simple but tasty apple cake.

Beef Burgundy
2 pounds of round steak
1 cup beef broth
1/2 cup burgundy or any good red wine
1 cup sliced mushrooms
Handful of parsley
3 tablespoons butter
3 tablespoons flour

Preheat oven to 425 degrees. Coat beef with flour, then bake uncovered in a lightly greased casserole dish for 20 minutes. Lower the oven temperature to 350 degrees. Add one cup of beef broth and 1/2 cup of any good red drinking wine. Cover and continue baking for one and one-half hours or until beef is tender. Add mushrooms and bake another 10 minutes adding additional broth or wine if needed. Meanwhile, melt 3 tablespoons of butter in a medium saucepan. Add 3 tablespoons of flour, stirring over medium heat until mixture begins to develop. Add pan juices and continue stirring until mixture blends and thickens. Add parsley and pour sauce over beef and serve over whole-wheat noodles, or alongside a heaping mound of mashed potatoes.

Apple Cake
1-3/4 cup sugar
2 cups flour
1 cup vegetable oil
1 tsp. baking soda
1/2 teaspoon salt
1 teaspoon cinnamon
1 teaspoon vanilla
4-5 apples sliced thin
1/2 cup raisins
3 eggs

Preheat oven to 350 degrees. Mix all of the above ingredients with a wooden spoon. Pour into ungreased 13x9-inch pan and bake 45 minutes. Serve warm with a dollop of whipped cream.

19

The Divine Whisper

The different ways God communicates to His followers

*Julie writes...*God talks to me. If I say it that simply, people don't understand me. They picture me sitting in my bedroom talking into the air and imagining some sort of reply. That's not quite the way it happens, but God truly communicates with me.

He speaks to me through His Word, the Holy Scriptures. Through the Bible, God reveals His requirements, expectations and His plan for me and for all of mankind. I also see His heart, His love, compassion, tenderness, and the limitless patience He displays to the most unruly, rebellious bunch ever created!

God speaks to me through the words of my pastor. It is the pastor's special job to be a conduit of communication from God to the members of a local church. Christians represent "the Body of Christ," *(1 Corinthians 12:12)*, and we are called to join together and function as a whole. *"Let us not give up meeting together, as some are in the habit of doing..." (Hebrews 10:25).* Gathered together in fellowship and worship in a local church presents a unique setting for God to speak to His people through their pastors.

Other Christians and church members can stand in for God too. Those believers who are well versed in the Scriptures can speak with authority as God's representatives. Whether our communication with other Christians is simply conversation, or if it comes closer to confrontation, encouragement, advice and counsel, it benefits us to listen to and consider the words of those who are known to have a "close walk" with the Lord.

Then there are the moments in my life when I hear what I like to call "the divine whisper." These are the moments when ideas come into my head that I haven't summoned. I remember the time I was overwhelmed with a church project, and a sudden thought streamed into my consciousness: "Why not ask Rita to help?" It was the farthest thought from my mind, yet it sprang up like the first bloom of spring. I have found that when I move on these inspired thoughts in faith, good things happen. Rita was delighted to lend a hand, commenting that she had more free time now and had been trying to think of a way to serve at church. I realized that God had spoken to each of us in different ways in order to both ease my workload and get Rita involved in the work He had for her.

The world is a visual place. God leaves signs for us everywhere. A friend lost her husband suddenly and tragically in an auto crash in 2004. She awoke the next morning to the sight of a flower that "happened" to bloom on a withered branch outside her window. It was past the season for it to bloom, and the flower, normally blue in color, was a pristine white. She recognized it as a symbol of comfort and peace, a sign left by her Heavenly Father.

News accounts some years ago carried the story of two American women who were arrested and jailed for spreading the gospel in Iran. For days on end they received no word from the U.S. Consulate or anyone else. They thought no one knew they were in prison. Then one of the young women caught a sign on the sanitary napkin packages their captors had provided. On the shelf were two brands, one named TRUST and one named ALWAYS. The idea of coincidence never entered their heads. They found peace and solace in this message of hope left for them by the God they loved who provided assurance to them that He was with them in their ordeal.

We become so used to the physical world that we can ignore the signs from God. Pay attention to the details in your life. What does God want to say to you today? The answers are found in the Bible, the words of God's people, the signs and wonders in the world around us...and in a still, small voice I like to call the "divine whisper."

Conversations at the Kitchen Table

- Have you ever sensed God speaking to you?

- Do you listen for that still, quiet voice in moments of decision-making?

- Can you identify ways in which God has guided your steps or sent His comfort in fearful moments or times of sorrow?

- The best way to hear God speak to you is by reading what He has to say about Himself and His plan for mankind in the pages of Scripture. If you don't have a Bible, purchase one of the more updated translations that are easier to read and spend some time with it each day.

- Don't expect instant intimacy with God. Ask Him to teach you His ways, and then spend some time each day sharing with Him what's on your heart. Read His word and let your ways, habits, attitudes and decisions be guided by what you read. Over time, you will sense His presence, see answers to prayer, develop greater confidence in His leadership, and find the source of your strength and the love of your life!

- Nothing else in life is more important than your relationship with God. If you're too busy to spend time with Him, you'll miss out on His best for your life! You can't hear Him if you don't spend quiet time in His presence. Dial down the noise in your life and let in some solitude. Feeling lonely? What better time to get away with God and ask Him to draw you into His presence? He speaks in *"a still, small voice…" (1 Kings 19:12 KJV)*, and if your life is a non-stop marathon, you risk forfeiting your own personal Promised Land! In *Psalm 46:10,* our Lord tells us *"Be still and know that I am God."*

Lavish "Be Still Before Him" Lunch

Tired of spinach yet? Good…we're not either!

Pasta and Vegetable Kugel with Cheese
1/4 cup butter
1 medium onion, peeled and minced
2 stalks celery, thinly sliced
1 red pepper, diced
1 package frozen, chopped spinach (thaw and squeeze dry)
10 ounces linguine
3 eggs
1 cup cottage cheese
1/2 cup sour cream
1 teaspoon fresh chopped basil
1/2 teaspoon paprika
Salt and pepper to taste
1/4 cup freshly grated Parmesan cheese

Preheat oven to 400 degrees. Sauté onions, celery and peppers in butter until soft. Add spinach and sauté several more minutes. Cook and drain pasta and transfer to a mixing bowl. Beat eggs and whisk in cottage cheese, sour cream and seasonings. Add cheese mixture and vegetables to pasta. Taste and adjust seasoning. Transfer mixture to buttered 13x9-inch baking dish. Sprinkle with Parmesan cheese and dust with additional paprika. Bake 25 minutes until firm. Let stand 5 minutes before serving.

Snow-capped Fudge Bars
Fudge Base
1 cup butter
4 squares unsweetened chocolate
3/4 cup sugar
3 eggs
1 cup flour
1/2 teaspoon salt
1 cup chopped walnuts
1 teaspoon vanilla extract

Topping
1 (8-ounce) package cream cheese
1 egg
1 teaspoon vanilla
5-6 drops Stevia (a natural, non-caloric, sweet-tasting alternative to sugar)

Preheat oven to 350 degrees. Melt butter and chocolate in a saucepan over low heat. Whisk in sugar and 3 eggs until blended. Stir in flour, salt, nuts and vanilla. Spread evenly in lightly-buttered 13x9-inch baking pan. In small bowl, beat cream cheese, egg, vanilla and Stevia. Drop cream cheese mixture in clumps on top of fudge base and spread evenly over pastry. Bake 25-30 minutes or until toothpick comes out clean. Be careful not to overbake! Cool and cut into bars.

20

He Will Direct Thy Steps

How to sense God's guidance in times of decision

*"Trust in the Lord with all your heart and lean not on your own understanding;
in all your ways acknowledge him, and he will make your paths straight."*

*A*rlene writes…This powerful promise is given to us in *Proverbs 3:5, 6.* Over the years, I have experienced God directing my steps in moments of decision. It has given me the confidence of knowing that the Lord is near, that He cares for me, and that He's willing to shape the contours of my life in matters great and small.

Some years ago I was about to turn down a job offer I wasn't sure was right for me. Before I could open my mouth to say no, a silent "yes" penetrated my thoughts, overruling my first inclination. I accepted the job having no way of knowing that God would use it to fulfill a number of my life long goals and dreams. On another occasion, I was meeting a friend for dinner I had not seen in a long time. Standing on the sidewalk in front of a maze of buildings looking for her new apartment, I decided I wasn't in the right place. I turned around to get back in my car when I suddenly felt compelled to halt, turn around and look up. I saw my friend waving frantically in an upstairs window trying to get my attention. When I finally got inside, she said, "It looked like you were going to drive away. What made you stop and turn around?" "I'm not really sure," I answered, "I just knew I had to take a second look before getting back in the car."

Years later, I had accumulated enough money for a down payment on a home. After months of looking, I found a house I liked. My bid was accepted and a day later, I felt that my insides had imploded. I was in a state of such restless anxiety that I could neither eat, sleep or work. I was filled with dread. After several days of this, I called and canceled the purchase. Immediately, peace flooded my being. In this instance, God was training me to rely on the Scripture, *"Let the peace of Christ rule in your hearts" (Colossians 3:15).*

When we trust God and put our lives in His hands, He will find many ways to alert and reveal to us the way in which we should proceed. It's been called the still, small voice, intuition, a gut check, an inner witness, a prompting of the Spirit. It is all these things and is more powerful and assured than any spoken word. We don't want to rush headlong into any decision without listening for it. It won't always make sense or it may even seem like a radical departure from our norm. It may scare us witless and call us to come miles out of our comfort zones. But when the prompting is from God, there's an unmistakable sureness and a peace that settles over us. *"I am the Lord your God, who teaches you what is best for you, who directs you in the way you should go"(Isaiah 48:17)*. God knows the way we should take. Trust in His divine providence, and the signpost will be there to meet us at every crossroad.

Conversations at the Kitchen Table

- Do you seek God's wisdom before making decisions? Always pray and seek His direction first. What may look and sound like a good thing now can end up being a disaster down the road. God knows the whole picture and to leave Him out of the equation will be to our detriment.

  The Lord confides in those who fear Him; He makes his covenant known to them (Psalm 25:14).

- Can you identify specific times in your life where God was directing your steps?

- In what way was it clear to you that it was a God-moment?

- Have some decisions resulted in a disruption of your peace that strongly signaled you were headed down the wrong path? In these instances, stop and seek God's direction. If it's possible, pull back and reverse course. Even when a bad decision you've made is irrevocable, however, don't fret and worry! Trust God to help you, knowing that *"...in all things God works for the good of those who love him, who have been called according to his purpose" (Romans 8:28).*

  "Stand at the crossroads and look; ask for the ancient paths, ask where the good way is, and walk in it, and you will find rest for your souls" (Jeremiah 6:16).

Lavish "Shining Path" Lunch

Here's a small step in a new direction: ditch the sodas and brew up a pitcher of our Raspberry-Apple refresher. As it chills, make a batch of our Date-Studded Banana Walnut cookies. While they're baking, whip up this easy, tasty, good-for-you salad. Enjoy lunch while you think of the ways God has guided you in the past and pray for Him to continue to intercede in your life.

Bulgur Salad with Carrots, Tomatoes and Chick Peas

1/2 cup cracked bulgur wheat
1/2 cup chicken broth
1 small cucumber, seeded and chopped
1 tomato, diced
1 carrot, shredded
1 cup chick peas
1/2 cup finely diced red onion
1 cup crumbled feta cheese
2-3 tablespoons fresh lime juice
1/4 cup chopped fresh parsley
1 teaspoon cumin
3/4 tablespoons chili powder
1/2 teaspoon garlic powder
Salt and pepper to taste

Place the bulgur in a colander and rinse under cold water. Drain and transfer to a small bowl. In a small saucepan, bring the chicken broth to a boil. Stir in the bulgur, remove from heat, and let stand for 40-45 minutes. Mix together cucumbers, tomatoes, shredded carrots, chick peas, red onion, feta cheese and parsley with the bulgur. Add lime juice and seasonings and toss. Serve with hummus and pita bread.

Date-Studded Banana Walnut Cookies

1/2 cup chopped dates
2/3 cup chopped walnuts
3 mashed bananas
2 cups oats
1/2 cup flaked coconut (optional)
1/2 cup vegetable oil
1 teaspoon vanilla

Preheat oven to 375 degrees. Combine all ingredients and drop by teaspoonful onto greased baking sheet. Bake 15-20 minutes.

Raspberry-Apple Refresher

4 cups spring or distilled water
2 raspberry herbal teabags

6 cups apple juice

Heat water and when barely trembling, remove from heat. Add teabags and let steep. Remove teabags and transfer tea to a pitcher. Add apple juice and serve over ice.

21

From A Seed to an Orchard:
the Principles of Sowing and Reaping

The boomerang law never varies: What we send out finds its way back

We make hundreds of decisions every day, most of them in a split second without much thought to their long-term effects. Good, bad or indifferent, one day we'll harvest those decisions. Maybe smoking looked cool in high school, then 20 years later, an x-ray shows lung damage…the visit to a casino with friends ends up draining the savings account to cover losses…a dare to try cocaine turns into a serious addiction…the sneak peak at a porn magazine becomes a daily obsession. What happened? A seemingly harmless decision ends up enslaving us. In his letter to the Galatians, the apostle Paul issues a dire warning to consider the long term, *"A man reaps what he sows"* (*Galatians 6:7*).

Natural laws are at work here. Just as gravity holds us firmly to the earth, the law of reaping and sowing is binding. When we plant potatoes, we harvest potatoes. Radishes will never sprout where we've planted green beans. If we sow anger, lust, greed, lies, pride or any other sinful seeds, a crop of harmful, destructive, poisonous, bitter fruit will spring forth. If that's been our crop up until now, God mercifully provides opportunities to plow over that worthless harvest and begin anew. *Lamentations 3:22, 23* tells us: *"…his compassions never fail. They are new every morning."*

In *Daniel 6* in the Old Testament, King Darius threw Daniel into the lions' den after a false accusation of disloyalty by the king's advisors. God intervened and shut the mouths of the lions, sparing Daniel, who was later vindicated. Once the king became aware of his advisors' treachery, he had them thrown into the lions' den along with their wives and children. They received the horrible death they had intended for Daniel. *"Be sure that your sin will find you out"* (*Numbers 32:23*).

Their lies and deceit not only came back on their own heads, but other innocents suffered the consequences. We are not islands set apart from one another. The decisions we make set a course for our lives and affect our families and loved ones.

In his letter to the Galatians, Paul tells us that we are called to sow fruits of the spirit: *"love, joy, peace, patience, kindness, goodness, faithfulness, gentleness and self-control" (Galatians 5:22)*. We are called to sow these fruits even when we've been hurt, betrayed, wronged or falsely accused. Christ's final hours leave us a blueprint for such grace under fire. *"He was oppressed and afflicted, yet he did not open his mouth; he was led like a lamb to the slaughter, and as a sheep before her shearers is silent, so he did not open his mouth" (Isaiah 53:7)*.

Later in his letter to the Galatians, Paul again cautions his listeners, *"The one who sows to please his sinful nature… will reap destruction; the one who sows to please the Spirit, from the Spirit will reap eternal life" (Galatians 6:8)*. And in a world where it sometimes seems that evil is rewarded while good is trampled and scorned, Paul encourages us to keep sowing good seeds even when the climate is harsh and the soil is rocky, *"Let us not become weary in doing good, for at the proper time we will reap a harvest if we do not give up" (Galatians 6:9)*.

Conversations at the Kitchen Table

- Do you see areas in your life where, for better or worse, you have sown and reaped?

- Does this message help you to see the importance of sowing good seeds?

- Have you taken any and all bad harvests before God in repentance and changed seed supply stores?

- Do you struggle with God when His direction doesn't seem to make sense? Read *Isaiah 55:8, 9* and *Proverbs 14:12*.

- There will be times when you attempt to do all the right things, yet nothing turns out the way you expect or hope. What's our response to these frustrating episodes when they occur? Let's take a look at *Romans 8:28*. *"And we know that in all things God works for the good of those who love him, who have been called according to his purpose."*

This verse assures us that even the hardships, difficulties, failures and disappointments are never dead ends, never wasted, never the end of life as we know it. Just as the grain of sand is an irritant that causes the oyster to form a pearl covering, God will translate our heartbreaks and setbacks into new weapons for our armor closets, bouquets of compassion for another trampled soul, a steel reinforcement that keeps us from a relapse and ready to face whatever life has to throw at us! With God at our side, life has no weapons against us!

Lavish "Harvester" Lunch

Today we're featuring a bumper crop of fruits and vegetables! We love combining foods for an interesting blend of colors, textures and tastes. These two don't disappoint! When making sweet potatoes for dinner, throw on a few extra to make our healthy, low-fat sweet treat below!

Red Potato ~ Green Bean Medley
4-5 red potatoes, quartered
2 cups fresh green beans, trimmed and cut in thirds
4 tablespoons extra virgin olive oil, divided
1 cup sliced mushrooms
1 small onion, diced
1 clove garlic, minced
1 (15-ounce) can diced tomatoes, undrained
1 (15-ounce) can garbanzo beans, drained
1 teaspoon Dijon mustard
Salt and pepper
1 tablespoon basil
1/4 cup fresh parsley

Boil potatoes for 15-20 minutes until fork tender; add green beans last four minutes. Drain and place in large bowl. Sauté mushrooms, onions, garlic in 2 tablespoons of olive oil and add to bowl along with beans and tomatoes. Combine remaining 2 tablespoons olive oil and Dijon mustard. Drizzle over salad and toss to combine. Season with salt and freshly-ground pepper, basil and parsley.

Sweet Potato~Pineapple Bake
3-4 sweet potatoes
1 (15 ounce) can crushed pineapple, undrained
1/4 cup brown sugar or honey
1/2 cup chopped walnuts

Preheat oven to 350 degrees. Bake sweet potatoes for one hour or until fork tender. When cooled, peel and mash with fork. Combine with crushed pineapple and brown sugar or honey. Add chopped walnuts and spoon into serving dish. Bake for 20-25 minutes. Serve warm or cold straight from the fridge.

22

Guard Your Heart with All Diligence

Be alert for the foxes out to destroy our gardens

Most of us are capable of committing an offense against God that shocks our sensibilities like a plunge into icy water. It could be a first-time sin, the likes of which we never thought ourselves capable. Perhaps it's the latest occurrence of sin that had us in bondage we thought we had finally conquered.

Whether it's a first or the latest in a long struggle to overcome, it's important to understand how it gained ground. Quite simply, we failed to guard our hearts. We need only look to King David, who became entranced with Bathsheba when, from his rooftop vantage, he saw her bathing *(2 Samuel 11)*. His desire for her led him to send for her, sleep with her and then have her husband killed in battle to cover up the adultery and resulting pregnancy.

These events are even more surprising since David was *"a man after God's own heart" (1 Samuel 13:14)*. How could David, who enjoyed God's favor and had such a resplendent history of victories in his journey with the Lord, be capable of committing such gross acts of wickedness? The same way we all are, by failing to heed the admonition, *"Above all else, guard your heart, for it is the wellspring of life" (Proverbs 4:23)*.

What was David doing on the rooftop? His army was out doing battle and his rightful place was to be with them leading the charge. But he had grown complacent, perhaps weary of warfare, feeling restless, and was absolutely ripe for the temptation that ambushed him. He was not where he should have been, and when his wandering eye caught the sight of a beautiful woman, he was utterly unprepared in that moment to wage warfare against the lust that arose in his heart. The consequences of that action were enormous, not only for him but for others as well.

Evil and wickedness are not exotic plants that grow on the opposite side of the world. They are common, everyday weeds that sprout in our own gardens. If we are not mindful of God's presence and in a watchful state for the enemy who *"prowls around like a roaring lion looking for someone to devour" (1 Peter 5:8)*, we too can get caught unawares and fall into sin we would never have imagined. It's as close as a thought, an unexpected desire and not acting quickly and forcefully enough to avert the eye from the forbidden.

David's story is a reminder that we must never let down our spiritual guard. Tiredness can easily become weariness that gives way to complacency. Stay alert because the enemy is close at hand. Continual refreshment is needed to maintain our strength and bear up under the struggles of life. That does not come by wandering around aimlessly on rooftops, but by daily meeting and fellowshipping with the Lord, the only true source of our strength.

"So if you think you are standing firm, be careful that you don't fall"
(1 Corinthians 10:12).

Conversations at the Kitchen Table

- Have you ever fallen into unexpected sin that caught you by surprise?

- Does this message help you to see the need to guard your heart daily?

- Can you identify areas of your life that need reinforcement to keep you from slipping? Work with your accountability partner to help keep you strong and able to fight off temptation.

- Pray for God's help over whatever may have you snared.

- The people we read about in the Bible are frail, fragile human beings shot through with faults and weaknesses just as we are. God did not withdraw His love from King David over this sin, but He did allow the consequences to take their deadly toll. When David was confronted with this sin, he was humbled, contrite and repentant. Read David's prayer of repentance in *Psalm 51*.

  "If we confess our sins, he is faithful and just and will forgive us our sins and purify us from all unrighteousness" (1 John 1:9).

Lavish "New Resolve" Lunch

Over lunch, think of one area in your life that needs work and resolve to make one small change to improve it. Less TV? Drink more water? Ten minutes a day with your Bible? Start small, be consistent and watch how this one small change will bring on other, greater changes! Hey, maybe eat more spinach? Works for us! This dish is versatile and can be packed into muffin tins, formed into pancakes, or baked in a casserole. Julie packs hers into heart shaped molds.

Spinach~Ricotta Cakes
2 (10-ounce) package frozen, chopped spinach
1 (8-ounce) container ricotta cheese
2 cups cooked brown rice
1 (12-ounce) jar marinated artichoke hearts, quartered
1/2 cup finely diced red pepper
3 egg whites, beaten until stiff
1/2 teaspoon salt
Dash pepper
1/8 teaspoon cayenne pepper
3-4 cloves chopped garlic (more if you're adventurous!)
1 cup crumbled feta cheese
1 cup bread crumbs (only if you're making into pancakes)
Creamy horseradish sauce

Thaw and squeeze spinach dry. Combine cooked rice with spinach, red pepper, artichoke hearts, seasonings, ricotta and feta cheeses. Gently fold in egg whites. To make muffins, mound into regular size muffin pans (use non-stick spray) and bake at 350 degrees for 15-20 minutes. To make pancakes, form into patties and roll in bread crumbs. Heat and coat a large skillet with extra virgin olive oil. Sauté each patty on both sides several minutes until crisp and golden. Another option is to transfer entire mixture into buttered 13x9-inch casserole dish and bake 30 minutes. However you make them, serve with sour cream horseradish sauce: 1 cup sour cream and 2 tablespoons horseradish.

Berries over Snow Pie
1 baked pie shell
1 (3-ounce) package of cream cheese, room temperature
1 quart fresh strawberries
3 tablespoons cornstarch
3/4 cup sugar
1 cup whipping cream

Clip stems from berries, wash, drain and slice. Meanwhile, beat cream cheese until smooth and spread over the bottom of the cooled pie shell. Place half of the strawberries over cream cheese layer in pie shell. Press the remaining berries through a strainer extracting the juice. Bring juice to boiling point and slowly add sugar and cornstarch. Cook 8-10 minutes stirring occasionally. Allow to cool before spooning over berries in shell. Chill and serve with whipped cream.

23

The Master Gardener

God knows how to replant our dry, barren fields

"Mary, Mary quite contrary, how does your garden grow?" is the only line we can recall from a childhood nursery rhyme. Webster's defines contrary as "opposite in purpose or direction; adverse, unfavorable, given to recalcitrant behavior, willful and perverse." Heartache, disappointment and adversity could well have caused bitter roots to sprout weeds in the garden of Mary's heart. Weeds are a blight with a destructive bent that can choke and crowd out the delicate flowers that grow alongside them.

This is a job for the Master Gardener. There's no renegade garden He can't uproot, recondition and return to a landscape of thriving blossoms. There's no tangled mass of killer weeds He can't dislodge, no matter what has happened to turn our hearts sour and bitter. Our situations may appear hopeless:

- We can't recover from our pile of mistakes
- We're backed into a corner with no way out
- We're too old and the clock has run out on any attempt to change the outcome of the game
- It's too late to undo the last 20, 30 or 50 years of our lives that have brought us to a fruitless end
- We've suffered too many losses and can't go on

These are lies our adversary wants to spoon-feed us that will rob us of hope and keep us on Spare-a-Penny Street. Allowing wretched thoughts like these to linger will plunge our spirits into a pit of despair. Satan is the "father of lies" and these are some of his most nefarious.

No matter how we've blown it or how much damage has been done, when we surrender our dry, barren field of weeds to God, He digs in. He'll use our pile-up of accumulated waste as fertilizer to cultivate, prune and bring forth a planting of exceptional, breathtaking beauty. Our lives will become stunning displays of His grace and truth that will attract crowds of admirers who come to view the grandeur of the Master Gardener's extraordinary skill.

Our beautiful, restored gardens will bring Him glory. Weary travelers will sit in the shade of our branches to recover from the scorching sun...others will smell the fragrance of our colorful blooms and breathe in new hope and confidence for the journey...still others will take courage from viewing this former garbage dump that has been transformed into a place of beauty. They'll leave refreshed knowing restoration is possible for them too.

"I am the true vine, and my Father is the gardener" (John 15:1).

"I am the vine; you are the branches. If a man remains in me and I in him, he will bear much fruit; apart from me you can do nothing" (John 15:5).

Conversations at the Kitchen Table

- Have you consulted with the Master Gardener on the state of your garden?

- Are there weeds in your garden so deep and widespread you feel your garden is beyond repair? That's what your adversary will tell you, but why don't we allow God to have His say! Please meditate on these Scriptures:

  "Forget the former things; do not dwell on the past. See, I am doing a new thing. Now it springs up; do you not perceive it? I am making a way in the desert and streams in the wasteland" (Isaiah 43:18, 19).

  "I will lead the blind by ways they have not known, along unfamiliar paths I will guide them; I will turn the darkness into light before them and make the rough places smooth. These are the things I will do; I will not forsake them" (Isaiah 42:16).

- Do these Scriptures help you to see that God never abandons us, kicks us to the curb, decides we're hopeless and refuses to have any more to do with us? He loves us with an everlasting love (*Jeremiah 31:3*) and will always be there in spite of our faithlessness, failures and flaws.

  "As a father has compassion on his children, so the Lord has compassion on those who fear him; for he knows how we are formed, he remembers that we are dust" (Psalms 103:13, 14).

- Read about some of the Bible characters whose lives were dramatically transformed: Ruth and Naomi in the book of Ruth

- Saul who became the apostle Paul in the book of Acts

- The fisherman Simon who became Peter, about whom Christ said *"on this rock I will build my church, and the gates of Hades will not overcome it"* (Matthew 16:18)

- Talk with your friends about people you know who have undergone godly transformations.

Lavish "Renewed Garden" Lunch

This is one of our favorite veggie dishes…colorful, nutritious and delicious! These mini-cups of pure bliss feature a truffle-like raspberry filling encased in a robe of chocolate—too fabulous!

Garden Veggie Medley
2 cups broccoli florets
2 cups cauliflower florets
2 carrots, sliced
2-3 tablespoons extra virgin olive oil
1 clove garlic, minced
1 cup sliced mushrooms
1 zucchini, diced
1 small onion, chopped
1 can diced tomatoes
1 can small white beans, drained
2 teaspoons basil
2 teaspoons oregano
1/4 cup chopped parsley
1 (8-ounce) package shredded Monterey Jack-cheddar cheese
Salt and pepper

Steam broccoli, cauliflower, and carrots for four minutes. Transfer to large mixing bowl. Sauté garlic, onions, mushrooms, and zucchini in olive oil, add to steamed veggies. Add tomatoes, beans, seasonings and cheese. Serve alone or with brown rice.

Chocolate~Raspberry Bite-of-Heaven
Dough
1 cup softened butter
1 cup powdered sugar
2 tablespoons unsweetened cocoa
1-3/4 cups flour
1 egg yolk

Cream butter and add remaining ingredients. Press dough on bottom and up the sides of mini-muffin cups. Bake 10 minutes at 350 degrees. Set aside to cool.

Filling
1 cup of chocolate chips
1 (8-ounce) package cream cheese, softened
1/3 cup seedless raspberry preserves
1/4 cup powdered sugar

Melt chocolate chips. Meanwhile beat together cream cheese and preserves with mixer. Beat in cooled melted chips and powdered sugar. Spoon filling into cooled chocolate cups. Chill several hours; bring to room temperature before serving.

24

Teacups and Tidal Waves

An equal or greater force is needed to repel a storm surge

⧡

*A*rlene writes…Recently I accompanied a friend to visit a former co-worker who was very depressed as she struggled with a number of life issues. Her husband had left her long ago, her children were grown and lived in other cities, and her company had just made the decision to let her go. She was alone in a house full of past memories and no new ones in the making.

We made tea and listened as she poured out her heart on the sadness and emptiness of her days that had once been full of people, purpose and activity. We spent hours praying with her, encouraging her, referencing countless uplifting Scriptures and suggesting a number of ways to get her life moving again. On that day, however, it was to no avail. "Well, thanks for trying," my friend said, as we drove home in the car, reflecting on the afternoon that had not elicited even a spark of hope. "At least you inspired me," she offered.

I was searching my heart and my head for pathways and Scriptures we had missed when I suddenly recalled myself in the not-so-distant past in my own living room in the same stressed out, miserable state as the woman we had just left. What had it taken for me to rise up out of that wreckage and forge a new path to abundant life? I knew it was the word of God…His promises, His hope, His assurances that no matter what abyss we fall into, He's ready with a lifeline to pull us out, shower us clean and get us moving again in the right direction. But one teacup full of God's word against a tidal wave of doubt, fear and hopelessness that's been building for weeks, months, or years won't get immediate results. An equal force of promise and hope is required to come against and overcome the power and strength of that storm surge of negativity.

The word of God is more powerful than any tidal wave that's about to hit our shores, but it's got to be applied in massive doses. We need the heavy artillery of *Psalms 23* and *91* to be applied morning, noon and night. If we don't even feel like dragging ourselves to church, we can ask a friend or neighbor to pick us up and go along. This is where a Bible study, small group, and accountability/prayer partners help immeasurably. They will come alongside to pray with us, encourage us, and lift us up when our spirits are flagging.

The Christian life is not a solo undertaking. There's no "Lone Ranger" Christianity. Jesus called the twelve and it's been a group undertaking since then.

> *"Two are better than one, because they have a good return for their work: If one falls down, his friend can help him up" (Ecclesiastes 4:9, 10).*

> *"All the believers were together and had everything in common. Selling their possessions and goods, they gave to anyone as he had need. Every day they continued to meet together in the temple courts. They broke bread in their homes and ate together with glad and sincere hearts, praising God and enjoying the favor of all the people" (Acts 2:44-47).*

Conversations at the Kitchen Table

- Where do you place yourself on the positive/negative thinking scale?

- If you're allowing your situation and circumstances to defeat you, the first step is to check your thoughts! If they're off roaming around in the wilderness, bring them back under the canopy of Scripture! God's word is true, eternal and our weapon of choice when we want to battle habitual, negative thought patterns.

   "As the rain and the snow come down from heaven, and do not return to it without watering the earth and making it bud and flourish, so that it yields seed for the sower and bread for the eater, so is my word that goes out from my mouth: it will not return to me empty, but will accomplish what I desire and achieve the purpose for which I sent it" (Isaiah 55:10, 11).

- Are you spending enough time with the *Light of the World* to shed light on your thought life?

   I am the light of the world. Whoever follows me will never walk in darkness, but will have the light of life (John 8:12).

   "...the kingdom of God is within you!"(Luke 17:21). Discuss with your friends what this verse means.

- Choose your thoughts carefully. They can take you to the heights or plunge you into the depths. When sadness, depression, irritation, anxiety or a sour mood strike, don't allow them to settle in! Challenge these rancid thoughts and fight them off with the word of God...align to your message pillars! Read *Ephesians 1:18-20* for an inspiring passage of Scripture that tells of the incomparably great power that resides in our spirits waiting to be accessed for our good and God's greater glory!

   "Many there be which say of my soul, 'there is no help for him in God.' But thou, O Lord, art a shield for me; my glory, and the lifter up of mine head"(Psalm 3:2, 3 KJV).

Lavish "Spot of Tea" Lunch

Today's lunch calls for an audience so invite over some friends or neighbors who will applaud your culinary skills. Since today's session refers to teacups, let's brew a pot of honey vanilla chamomile tea to accompany these raspberry scones.

Crab Florentine
6 ounces fresh or 1 (6 ounce) can crabmeat
1/2 cup fresh mushrooms, sliced
2 tablespoons butter
1 (10-ounce) package frozen spinach (thaw and squeeze dry)
4 eggs
1 cup sour cream
1 cup cottage cheese
1 cup grated Parmesan cheese
1/3 cup flour
Pinch of salt and freshly ground pepper
1 cup shredded mozzarella cheese

Sauté mushrooms in butter until tender. Place in bowl with drained spinach. In a blender or food processor, mix eggs, sour cream, cottage cheese, Parmesan cheese, flour, salt and pepper. Fold in mushrooms, spinach, crabmeat and cheese. Spoon into greased 10-inch springform pan. Bake 45 minutes at 350 degrees or until golden on top and knife inserted in center comes out clean. Let rest five minutes before serving.

Raspberry Scones
1-3/4 cups all purpose-flour
1 cup sweetened flaked coconut
1/2 cup white chocolate chips, chopped (optional, but go for it!)
1/4 cup sugar
1 tablespoon baking powder
1 tablespoon grated lemon zest
1/2 teaspoon salt
3/4 cup heavy cream
2 large eggs
2 cups fresh raspberries or 1 (10-ounce) package frozen raspberries
2 tablespoons sugar

Preheat oven to 375 degrees. Coat a baking sheet with non-stick spray. Mix together the flour, coconut, white chocolate, sugar, baking powder, lemon zest and salt. In small bowl, whisk cream and eggs. Pour over flour mixture; add berries and stir just until mixed and dough clumps together. Place dough on a cookie sheet and form into a 9-inch round shape, and sprinkle with sugar. Coat a knife with nonstick spray and cut 8 wedges into unbaked mixture (don't separate at the bottom). Bake 30-35 minutes until a toothpick comes out clean. Serve warm.

25

The Silent Corrosion of Sin
Never downplay its acidic effects

*A*rlene writes…I remember frolicking for hours on the shore of Lake Tahoe in my teen years, oblivious to the damaging rays of the sun. The next day I woke up horrified to see a fiery brick-red face staring back at me from the mirror. Day One I passed out in the hallway of our vacation home, weak and shivering. Day Five I was blistered and peeling…with half-new/half-burned skin, looking like someone in the final stages of leprosy.

I wish I could tell you I never had sunburn again. It's more than a challenge to protect ourselves from something that's with us nearly every day. Do you see where we're going with this? Sin is a lot like that…its corrosive effects are not always immediately visible. We're having a good time totally unaware that it's silently wreaking horrible damage in some area of our lives. *"The wages of sin is death"* says *Romans 6:23*. Very few people want to talk about sin and the road to perdition – otherwise known as hell. There are fewer still that even believe it's a real place.

Christ, however, minced no words in addressing it in *Mark 9:43:" If your hand causes you to sin, cut it off, it is better for you to enter life maimed than with two hands to go into hell."* He gave the same instructions regarding our foot and our eye. He describes hell as a real place where *"their worm does not die and the fire is not quenched" (Mark 9:48).*

Sin in our lives may well go undetected over the course of a lifetime. This can easily cause us to adopt a false sense of security since no one has noticed. Make no mistake, however, God notices. *"Nothing in all creation is hidden from God's sight. Everything is uncovered and laid bare before the eyes of him to whom we must give account" (Hebrews 4:13).* In Christ we have new natures and sin loses its grip on us. However, we still live in fleshly bodies in a sin-prone world and we're not immune from temptation.

Very early in my work life, I pilfered a three-ring binder and sheet protectors from the office to hold my growing recipe collection. I rationalized there were scads in the supply closet that weren't being used, plus it saved me a trip to the office supply store. One day I left the binder too close to the burner on my gas range when I was cooking dinner. My smoke detector blared out a warning. I turned to find flames licking its spine, leaving it scorched and smoking, its cover burned and blotched. What I thought a harmless indulgence in taking what wasn't mine, God clearly thought otherwise. I still have the binder as a visual reminder of the corrosive effects of sin. *"the little foxes… ruin the vineyard"(Song of Songs 2:15).*

To covet, to lust, to be envious, jealous, greedy, adulterers, liars, thieves…these are worldly passions that no longer match our identities as new creatures in Christ. In *2 Corinthians 5:17* we learn *"If anyone is in Christ, he is a new creation; the old has gone, the new has come."* We step out of the quicksand, but some of it still clings even as we walk in our newness of life. Rest assured, however, we'll get the memo for our next clean-up assignment. Hopefully no smoke alarms will be involved!

> *"And if on some point you think differently, that too God will make clear to you.*
> *Only let us live up to what we have already attained" (Philippians 3:15, 16).*

Conversations at the Kitchen Table

- Does this message help you see the need to regularly take a spiritual inventory and clean out the closets?

- Have you casually tolerated certain sins to later discover the silent, hidden damage they caused?

- It's easy to rationalize some sins and think they're not serious enough to warrant the effort to root them out. That's why it's important to adopt God's view of sin. He took it so seriously that He sent His Son Jesus to sacrifice His life to pay our sin debt. *"But he was pierced for our transgressions, he was crushed for our iniquities; the punishment that brought us peace was upon him, and by his wounds we are healed. We all, like sheep, have gone astray, each of us has turned to his own way; and the Lord has laid on him the iniquity of us all"* (Isaiah 53:5, 6).

- Read and reflect on the following Scriptures that reveal the destructive consequences of sin:

Isaiah 5:20-24
Psalm 11:4-6
Proverbs 1:20-33
Proverbs 6:12-15

- If you are struggling with a long-standing, deeply-rooted sin, pray and ask God to get to the bottom of it so that it can be dislodged at the roots. Is that accountability partner on the job yet?

Lavish "Stay on the Sunny Side of the Street" Lunch

The simple yet noble bean stars in today's lavish lunch. Beans are packed with nutrition and so easy to add to soups, stews and casseroles of any kind. Since we're Michigan girls, we couldn't pass up the opportunity to provide a sweet treat using our famed tart cherries!

Spinach, Beans and Rice Casserole
1 can kidney beans, drained
1 can Northern beans, drained
1 (10-ounce) package chopped, frozen spinach (thaw and squeeze dry)
2 cups fresh green beans, trimmed and cut in bite-size pieces
1 tablespoon extra virgin olive oil
1 cup sliced mushrooms
1 small onion, diced
1 clove garlic, minced
1 can diced tomatoes, undrained
2 teaspoons basil
2 teaspoons oregano
1/4 cup chopped parsley
2 cups cooked wild rice blend
1/2 cup freshly-grated Parmesan cheese

Drain Northern beans and place in a large mixing bowl. Steam spinach and green beans for four minutes and add to Northern beans. Sauté garlic, onions and mushrooms in olive oil and add to mixing bowl. Add tomatoes, seasonings and cooked brown rice. Serve with Parmesan cheese.

Chocolate-Cherry Cookies
1/2 cup butter
1 cup sugar
1 egg
1-1/2 teaspoons vanilla
1-1/2 cups all purpose flour
1/2 cup cocoa
1/4 teaspoon baking powder
1/4 teaspoon baking soda
1/4 teaspoon salt
1 cup dried Michigan cherries
1 cup chocolate chips

Preheat oven to 350 degrees. Cream butter, sugar, egg and vanilla in a large mixing bowl until light and fluffy. Combine flour, cocoa, baking powder, soda and salt. Gradually add to creamed mixture until blended. Stir in cherries and chocolate chips. Drop by teaspoonfuls onto greased cookie sheet. Bake 8-10 minutes or until edges are set.

26

Blanch~Shock~Dry~Freeze–
What Herbs and Salvation Have in Common
Never put it past us to pair food and Scripture!

A noted chef on TV recently described a four-step method to save fresh herbs for winter use:

1. Blanch in boiling water
2. Shock in an icy bath
3. Remove and dry
4. Freeze and store

When they come out of the freezer for use in the winter months, their flavor will be as fresh and potent as when you picked them from the garden. Now, this may be a stretch for you, but we got the biggest kick out of thinking how much it reminded us of the process of salvation.

Follow us on this: Some people come to salvation in a long, slow process where they're drawn to the Savior over time. For others, however, it comes in an instant…much like saving fresh herbs. A person is thrown in a hot water situation where they have no earthly means of rescue…they're shocked into the realization that they need the God they've long denied… they're gently lifted out and cloaked in Christ's coat where they're kept safe and dry. Then they're frozen…or marked and sealed with the Holy Spirit until the day of their redemption. When they reengage the world, their testimony is vivid and potent, infusing a savory taste and aroma that enriches the dry repast of the tired lives and weary hearts they encounter.

Oh, come on! Pairing food and Scripture is what we do!

"You are the salt of the earth" (Matthew 5:13).

"Let your conversation be always full of grace, seasoned with salt, so that you may know how to answer everyone" (Colossians 4:6).

155

Conversations at the Kitchen Table

- Has a "hot water" situation made you realize your need for Christ?

- If so, have you carved out time to meet with Him daily? When you get a distress call from a close friend, you probably move heaven and earth to try and help. If the distress call is from an on-again-off-again, check-in-with-you-once-in-awhile kind of acquaintance, you can't help but wonder why this person only calls you in a crisis. Is that person really your friend if that's the only time you get a call? God feels the same way. He wants to be the first point of contact when a crisis looms, but He doesn't want to be left on the sidelines during the routines of life.

- Reading Scripture, talking to God, sitting silently in His presence, keeping a prayer journal are all good ways to stay in touch with God. When we get a sense of His presence on a daily basis, we won't go a day without it!

- Another key element in staying in the presence of God is to memorize some "message pillars" from Scripture that will keep you focused and grounded in God's word, His promises, His mandates and His direction. "*Whether you turn to the right or to the left, your ears will hear a voice behind you, saying, 'This is the way, walk in it'*" (*Isaiah 30:21*). This won't be an audible voice, but rather a thought that seems to come out of nowhere, a prompting, and a visceral sense of the right way to proceed.

- If you're honest, is it true that most days you just don't feel like praying or reading the Bible? It's a common problem and our advice to you is: Get over it! Think about it: the Great I Am, the Most High God, the Lord of all creation, your Heavenly Father, the one who flung the universe into being, the Limitless, Self-Existing, Eternal God wants to fellowship with you!! What could possibly take priority over that? Don't allow a lazy, "I'd rather shop, watch TV or gab on the phone" mentality rob you of the blessings of spending time with the God and Father of our Lord Jesus Christ!

- Read *Exodus 34:29-35*. What did Moses experience when he spent time in the presence of God?

- Read *Acts 4:13*. What change took place in the Apostles Peter and John by spending time with Jesus?

- Read *2 Corinthians 3:18*. What does this verse say we will experience by spending time with God?

Lavish "Hidden Flavor" Lunch

We had to have an herb play a leading role in today's menu. Our basil-based pesto is a great appetizer with pita bread. It can also be added to soups, salads, sauces or as an accompaniment to chicken or fish. Try substituting spinach or kale for the basil to up the nutritional value.

Homemade Pesto with Angel Hair Pasta
10 ounces angel hair pasta
1-1/2 cups pesto
1/2 cup Parmesan cheese
Options: tomatoes, mushrooms, veggies, leftover meat or chicken, sour cream

Pesto
3 ounces Parmesan cheese, cut in pieces
2 cloves garlic
3 cups packed fresh basil leaves, washed and dried
4-5 tablespoons extra virgin olive oil
5 tablespoons walnuts
1/4 teaspoon salt

In blender or food processor, process Parmesan cheese and garlic until cheese is crumbly. Add basil and process, 15-20 seconds. Add olive oil and process another 5 seconds until blended. Add walnuts, salt and process another 15-20 seconds. Refrigerate until ready to use.

Prepare pasta per package directions. Drain and toss with pesto and serve with additional Parmesan cheese. If you like, add diced tomatoes, sautéed mushrooms, steamed veggies or any leftover meat or chicken on hand from the previous day. For a creamier dish, mix pesto with one cup of sour cream before tossing with pasta.

Twin Nut Wonders
Is this a great name or what? And wait until you try them! These sweet, tender treats were included in a homemade recipe collection tied together with yarn that a long ago friend or acquaintance gave to Arlene's mom as a Christmas gift.

1/2 cup butter
3 tablespoons confectioner's sugar
1 cup flour
1 cup ground almonds
1 cup chocolate chips
1 cup pistachio nuts, ground

Preheat oven to 350 degrees. Cream together butter and sugar. Sift in the flour, then stir in almonds. Wrap and chill one hour. Form tablespoons of dough into two-inch thick logs. Cut in half lengthwise and place cut side down on cookie sheet. Bake 8-10 minutes until bottom edges are golden brown. Melt chocolate chips and frost rounded side of log. Generously sprinkle ground pistachios over chocolate. Recipe makes two dozen.

27

Holiness – Clean Hearts before God
Bears no resemblance to Suzy self-righteous

Today's topic is holiness. Now stick with us and don't turn the page! This might be a good time to get the teapot bubbling for a soothing cup of cinnamon-apple tea. If your first thoughts were "Holiness is asking too much," or "No thanks, that's like self-righteous Suzy next door, and who'd want to be like her?" … relax, sip some tea and keep reading.

First, holiness is asking too much if we think we can get there on our own, and second, God has no desire that we mimic Suzy self-righteous. She thinks too highly of herself, a deadly form of pride, and she needs to go back to square one. What is holiness? It's best described as having clean, pure hearts before God. *"Who may ascend into the hill of the Lord? Who may stand in his holy place? He who has clean hands and a pure heart, who does not lift up his soul to an idol or swear by what is false" (Psalm 24:3, 4).*

Marvin R. Wilson in *Our Father Abraham* states it beautifully: "It is the challenge for human beings to elevate all of life so that at each place, each hour, in each act and each speech, the holy can blossom forth."

Okay, we see this is what God desires for us. So…how do we get to a place where we're serving Him with clean hands and heart? As usual, God does the heavy lifting. First He awakens or draws us, then paints the canvas of our souls with the blood of His Son, blotting out our transgressions. Then He places the Holy Spirit in our hearts to help us facilitate needed changes. We are then cleansed, dressed and ready for service: *"He has committed to us the message of reconciliation. We are therefore Christ's ambassadors, as though God were making his appeal through us" (2 Corinthians 5:19, 20).*

A friend once said that Christians are the only "Bible" some people will ever read. That is why it's so important that we reflect Christ in our daily affairs. In the ongoing drama of our lives, God produces and directs; now we take the stage: *"But in your hearts set apart Christ as Lord. Always be prepared to give an answer to everyone who asks you to give the reason for the hope that you have. But do this with gentleness and respect" (1 Peter 3:15).*

Over time, through Bible study and reflection, daily prayer and a life mission of pursuing God, we will be transformed to the point where *"we have the mind of Christ" (1 Corinthians*

2:16). How stellar is that? To think, act, and behave in all ways as Christ would! Sounds like living holy before God really is in reach; and it doesn't call to mind anything like self-righteous Suzy, does it? Come to think of it…let's invite her over for tea!

> *"Put away the strange gods that are among you, and be clean, and change your garments" (Genesis 35:2).*

> *"Since we have these promises, dear friends, let us purify ourselves from everything that contaminates body and spirit, perfecting holiness out of reverence for God"(2 Corinthians 7:1).*

Our Father Abraham, Jewish Roots of the Christian Faith, by Marvin R. Wilson, 1989, William B. Eerdmans Publishing Company, Grand Rapids, Michigan and Center for Judaic-Christian Studies, Dayton, Ohio, p. 158.

Conversations at the Kitchen Table

- We hope Suzy will see that self-righteousness has no place in the heart of a child of God. No one can meet God's standard of perfection, "*...for all have sinned and fall short of the glory of God" (Romans 3:23)*. He looks upon our self-righteous acts as "*filthy rags" (Isaiah 64:6)*. That's why Christ is the only one who could stand in the gap for us!

  "The greatest among you will be your servant. For whoever exalts himself will be humbled, and whoever humbles himself will be exalted" (Matthew 23:11, 12).

- Does this message help you to see that living holy before God is not something we do on our own? First, God causes us to see our need for Christ. Then we place our full confidence and trust in Him to do the work in us that needs to be done.

  "For it is God who works in you to will and to act according to his good purpose" (Philippians 2:13).

  "Now it is God who makes both us and you stand firm in Christ. He anointed us, set his seal of ownership on us, and put his Spirit in our hearts as a deposit, guaranteeing what is to come"(2 Corinthians 1:21, 22).

  "But now He has reconciled you by Christ's physical body through death to present you holy in his sight, without blemish and free from accusation..." (Colossians 1:22).

- Can you sense the Holy Spirit in your life helping you to make course corrections? See *John 16:13, 14.*

- Discuss with your friends some small, simple ways you can elevate your everyday life to honor God. It could be a decision to cast off a sour mood and replace it with sweetness...refusing to rehash someone's criticism of you and say a prayer for them instead... helping a child master a skill...taking lunch or dinner over to someone who's ill or a new mom, opening your home for a Bible study. There are many ways in a day to be a light in this darkening world!

Lavish Lunch with Suzy

Since tea with Suzy went well, have her back for this lavish lunch! She will be delighted with this luscious Eggplant Parmesan and scrumptious Butter Cookies to serve with tea. If you've never worked with eggplant, give it a try! This recipe takes a little more prep time, but you'll have enough left over for a late supper or to freeze for another day.

Eggplant Parmesan
2 medium eggplants, ends removed, peeled and cut lengthwise in 1/4-inch slices
2 cups flour
4 beaten eggs
2 cups seasoned bread crumbs
Extra virgin olive oil

Cheese Filling
1 (15-ounce) carton ricotta cheese
1 (15-ounce) carton cottage cheese
2 beaten eggs
1 (8-ounce) package mozzarella

Tomato Sauce
2 (28-ounce) cans crushed tomatoes with Italian seasoning

Prepare cheese filling in mixing bowl, place crushed tomatoes in separate mixing bowl and set aside. Peel and slice eggplant. Arrange 3 additional bowls near the stove: one with flour, the next with eggs and the third with breadcrumbs. Heat a large skillet with olive oil. Dip each eggplant slice first in flour, then egg mixture, then coat with breadcrumbs. Sauté several eggplant slices at a time in skillet until both sides are golden adding olive oil to pan as needed. Drain on paper towels.

In a 13x9-inch baking dish, ladle 3-4 tablespoons of tomato sauce on bottom, top with one layer of eggplant, then spoon cheese mixture over eggplant. Add another layer of sauce, eggplant and cheese and finish with a topping of sauce. Sprinkle casserole with 1/4 cup of Parmesan cheese. Bake for 50-60 minutes at 350 degrees until hot and bubbly. Remove from oven and let stand for 15 minutes to set. Serve with tossed green salad.

Butter Cookies with Three-Way Frosting
1 cup butter
1/3 cup confectioner's sugar
3/4 cup cornstarch
1-1/4 cups sifted all purpose flour
1 cup finely chopped nuts

Preheat oven to 350 degrees. In a large mixing bowl, cream together butter and sugar. Blend in cornstarch and flour until ingredients are combined. Shape into 1-inch balls and roll in nuts. Place on greased cookie sheets and flatten with a fork. Bake for 12-15 minutes. Cool and top with a frosting that can deliver three different coats.

Three-Way Frosting
1-1/2 cups powdered sugar
Splash orange juice
Splash lemon juice
Splash cherry juice

Divide powdered sugar into three small bowls. Add lemon juice to one bowl, orange juice to second bowl and cherry juice to third bowl. Mix well, adding more juice if necessary until creamy and easy-to-spread. They look wonderful on a serving plate!

28

Murmuring Short-Circuits Our Blessings
Carping and complaining leaves us parched in the desert

Murmuring … we do it all the time in a variety of places and circumstances: boo/hiss, gripe/snipe, lament/resent, blame/complain… endlessly! We top each other with stories of how awful it's been: traffic was snarled, the movie was lame, our coffee got cold and the waitress went AWOL. The flight was canceled, the bagels ran out, the laptop crashed and the files weren't stored.

It's enough to make us wish we had stayed home. That's precisely how the children of Israel responded as they encountered one hardship after another in the desert as God led them from bondage in Egypt to the Promised Land in Canaan. On their way from backbreaking slavery under Pharaoh to a land of milk and honey, they saw fit to complain, whine and rebel. While God fed them with manna from heaven, served as expert tour guide and performed miracles along the way, the Spartan conditions of the desert journey caused many of them to regret leaving their lives as slaves in Egypt!

In *Exodus 16*, we read of Moses struggling to maintain his sanity against the constant carping, criticism and blame the Israelites laid at his feet when the VIP treatment they expected didn't quite materialize. In *Exodus 32*, we see Moses pleading for their lives when, in his absence, they engaged in idolatrous revelry. While he was alone with God receiving the Ten Commandments, they grew restless and bored and threw a wild party for their "new god," a golden calf. How quickly they forgot all that God had done for them! Their ingratitude, unfaithfulness and "what have you done for me lately" attitude roused the Lord's anger and a number of them died that day in the desert. Many lives were cut short before they could set foot upon the land of milk and honey…the land that had been promised to them. Their ungrateful hearts short-circuited their blessings.

We murmur too. As Americans, we are blessed beyond measure. We live as a free people with access to the best that life offers: an abundance of food, housing, education, a choice of professions. Yet we complain…about the weather, our jobs, incomes, spouses, children, homes and neighborhoods. We are never satisfied. God undoubtedly sighs and would no doubt roll His eyes heavenward if He weren't already there.

In the meantime, He patiently waits for us to recognize that it's time for us to leave Egypt too. He stands by waiting to lead us to our promised land. First, however, we have to let go of whatever is holding us captive, to want freedom in Christ so much that whatever meager pleasure we find in slavery is not worth sacrificing the land of milk and honey.

The road to freedom is never a cakewalk, not for the children of Israel and not for us. We have to want it enough to follow God across the dry, burning desert … not as malcontents and rebels, but with grateful hearts and thanksgiving for His every provision. Come on…our promised land awaits!

Conversations at the Kitchen Table

- Has complaining become so much of a backdrop to your life that you no longer hear it? *See Philippians 2:14-16.*

- Is it helpful to see that complaining is wasted energy that can be transformed into prayer that can deliver solutions?

- Do you have complaint partners that can be refashioned into prayer and praise partners? Perhaps the next time a friend brings up a litany of complaints, you can offer to pray for this person. Identify a Scripture for them to take before God, and tell them you will also make a commitment to keep that in your prayer time. This might be a good time to also suggest that they begin a prayer journal. Tell them about yours and how much it has blessed you! Check in with them every so often to see how things are going and continue to be an encouragement!

- Is it reasonable to praise God while suffering affliction and going through trials and difficulties? See the following Scriptures:

Psalm 34:2
Acts 16:22-25
Romans 5:1-5
2 Corinthians 6:3-10

Lavish "Sweetness and Light" Lunch

Welcome to the Promised Land! Today's menu features milk and honey, of course! We're serving up Honey-Mustard Chicken that will go nicely with grilled veggies or a crisp, green salad. Berry-Banana Milkshakes double as dessert and a beverage.

Honey-Mustard Chicken

4 boneless skinless chicken breast halves
2 tablespoons honey
1 tablespoon Dijon mustard
Sprinkle of salt and pepper

Heat oven to 350 degrees. Place the chicken in a greased 13x9-inch baking dish. Combine honey and Dijon mustard and brush over chicken breasts. Bake uncovered for 30 minutes. Place under broiler for four minutes to add a golden sheen. Serve alongside garlic mashed potatoes.

Berry-Banana Milkshakes

1 cup low-fat milk
1 cup freshly-squeezed orange juice
2 cups fresh or frozen berries (strawberries, raspberries, blackberries or mixture)
2 bananas

Puree ingredients in a blender and serve immediately.

29

Authenticity: Unmasking the Real You
When we wish we were someone else

At one time or another we've all wished we were someone else. We heard about, read about or observed someone else's life that seemed so much happier, more successful, exciting or exotic than ours and wished we had been born them instead of us. If that's been the case a little more often than we care to let on, then it's time to get to work. First, let's identify the malaise. What's missing that's causing us to wistfully imagine ourselves in someone else's shoes? Have some hopes gone up in flames…have some dreams evaporated…have some goals fallen by the wayside?

Granted, some things may have slipped beyond our reach. If we've already celebrated our 40th birthdays, dreams of rocketing to Mars, becoming a heart surgeon or winning an Olympic medal may have to be scratched from the list. But other dreams are still waiting for us to catch hold of and bring to the light of day. There's plenty left to achieve and stir excitement in our souls when we wake up in the morning.

Chronic discontentment and the feeling that something is missing is a strong sign that we're not on the path God intended for us. God created us to be exactly who we are…in this very time and place on the flowchart of eternity. We are unique…originals… individual masterpieces. Each of us is an imaginative spark that streamed from the mind of a creative, brilliant-beyond-our-imagination Creator. At conception, we were fully packaged with gifts and abilities waiting to be unveiled. *"All the days ordained for me were written in your book before one of them came to be" (Psalm 139:16)*. God wants to see us come fully into our own genuine, authentic, not-like-anyone-else personas.

Since each of us is *"fearfully, wonderfully made" (Psalm 139:14)*, we should never sell ourselves short. We just need to get busy discovering the gifts He's endowed us with and start to develop and utilize them for His glory. With the divine spark that is innate within us, great things can and should be displayed in the tapestry of our lives. God thinks so! Scripture tells us that our work will be tested: *"It will be revealed with fire, and the fire will test the quality of each man's work" (1 Corinthians 3:13)*. Don't let this test make you anxious. Trust God and leave the outcome to Him. *"But he knows the way that I take; when he has tested me, I will come forth as gold" (Job 23:10).*

Each one of us is irreplaceable. No one else can live the life each of us was designed to live…to serve God in our time, our circle and sphere of influence. Created in His image and likeness, *Genesis 1:26,* has all the makings for us to live far above and beyond the ordinary, the mundane! *"No eye has seen, no ear has heard, no mind has conceived what God has prepared for those who love him…but God has revealed it to us by his Spirit"(1 Corinthians 2:9-10).*

Who would want to be anybody else? Let's get joyfully busy being exactly the one God created us to be! We've got a final exam somewhere up ahead…but not to worry, the Holy Spirit has been assigned as our tutor, and He gets guaranteed results!

> *"But the Counselor, the Holy Spirit, whom the Father will send in my name, will teach you all things and will remind you of everything I have said to you"(John 14:26).*

Conversations at the Kitchen Table

- Have you ever wished you were someone else?

- Does this message help you to see that God knew exactly what He was doing when He created you for His glory?

  "My frame was not hidden from you when I was made in the secret place. When I was woven together in the depths of the earth, your eyes saw my unformed body. All the days ordained for me were written in your book before one of them came to be" *(Psalms 139:15, 16).*

  "I know, O Lord, that a man's life is not his own; it is not for man to direct his steps" *(Jeremiah 10:23).*

- Do you have unrealized goals and dreams that you want to bring to the light of day? Read *Psalm 37:4.* Will you commit to setting time aside to bring them before God on a daily basis and ask for His help in bringing them to pass? Remember, if your dreams/ visions are not according to God's plan, He will still use your prayers to align your dreams and visions with His will.

- Don't make the mistake of thinking your dream must not be from God if you encounter obstacles, trials and hardship in bringing it to reality. Read the story of Joseph in *Genesis 37* to *47.* Joseph had dreams and visions given to him by God but he had to undergo much heartache, betrayals, exile, false accusations and imprisonment before his dreams came to fruition. God was at work behind the scenes throughout Joseph's many ordeals, but it took tremendous patience, faith, trust and endurance for Joseph to hold on to his dreams and not grow bitter.

Lavish "Glad to Be Me" Lunch

Our Zucchini/Potatoes with Salsa can be served as a main dish or a side. Leftovers can be paired with shredded, cooked chicken and wrapped in tortillas…add some sour cream and avocado and you've got the makings for an instant fiesta! Cool things down with our luscious peaches and cream parfaits…healthy, delicious and beautiful sitting on a sideboard waiting to be presented to your special guests!

Zucchini and Potatoes with Salsa

4-6 potatoes, peeled and quartered
1-2 tablespoons extra virgin olive oil
2-3 small zucchini, cut in cubes
1 onion, halved, then quartered and sliced in strips
1 green, red or yellow pepper diced (or half of a combo package of all three)
2 garlic cloves, minced
1 small can diced green chilies
1/2 teaspoon cumin
1/8 teaspoon red pepper flakes
1 teaspoon dried thyme
1 teaspoon dried oregano
1 bunch cilantro, chopped
1 jar homemade or favorite store-bought salsa
1 (8-ounce) package shredded Mexican blend cheese
Salt and pepper to taste

Boil potatoes in pan of lightly salted water and cook about 15 minutes until fork tender. Drain and set aside. Coat a skillet with olive oil and lightly sauté zucchini, onions, peppers and garlic. In a mixing bowl, cut potatoes into chunks, add zucchini mixture along with diced green chilies and salsa. Add seasonings and toss with cheese.

Peaches and Cream Parfaits

6 large fresh peaches (reserve two for topping)
1 (32-ounce) carton plain yogurt, drained
1 cup heavy or whipping cream
Stevia (non-caloric, natural alternative to sugar)
1/2 cup finely chopped walnuts
1/2 cup granola
2 cups heavy cream

A day ahead or the morning of your lunch, place yogurt in cheesecloth and set in a strainer inside a bowl to drain in refrigerator. Meanwhile, beat heavy or whipping cream until stiff peaks form. Add several drops of Stevia to sweeten. Peel and puree 4 peaches in a blender and mix with drained yogurt. In a separate bowl, combine walnuts and granola. When ready to assemble, spoon a generous tablespoon of the sweetened yogurt-peach cream into bottom of four parfait glasses. Add a tablespoon of the walnut-granola mixture followed by a swirl of whipped cream, then a tablespoon of reserved peaches, cut as desired. Continue to layer until glasses are full. Finish with whipped cream and a sprinkling of granola.

30

The Importance of Being Earnest
Living with purpose means matching words to deeds

We say things and make commitments all the time we don't mean, have no intention of carrying out and thoroughly dismiss the second the words pass our lips. We don't realize it means we're not being truthful, or that we don't live intentionally. Even worse, we don't think it matters! To live intentionally, however, is to live purposefully, supported by words that convey that intention and purpose.

The most common of these "true lies" is the innocuous social jargon in which we engage. "Let's have lunch sometime…we really should get together…I'll call you soon to make plans …" serve as quick but meaningless conversation closers when we run into acquaintances, long-lost friends, former co-workers, neighbors and even family members. Sometimes we're aware before the words are even out of our mouths that it's not going to happen. We may sincerely want to carve out a time and place to spend with that person, but our casual commitment is quickly swamped in the ebb and flow of our busy lives.

We're no different when it comes to God. We listen to His instructions, nod our heads in agreement, then turn and wander far afield. It's not the kind of paradox He likes to see in His children: *"These people come near to me with their mouth and honor me with their lips, but their hearts are far from me" (Isaiah 29:13).*

We have good intentions. It's recorded somewhere that the road to hell is paved with them. Words alone communicate no resolve. It's the actions that follow that unmask the heart's true intent. In *The Parable of the Two Sons*, in *Matthew 21:28-31*, Jesus tells the story of a man who went to his first son and said, " 'Son, go and work today in the vineyard.' 'I will not,' he answered, but later he changed his mind and went. Then the father went to the other son and said the same thing. He answered 'I will, sir,' but he did not go. 'Which of the two did what his father wanted?' Jesus asked. 'The first,' they answered."

Luke 3:8 tells us to *"produce fruit in keeping with repentance."* Half truths, white lies, forgotten commitments no longer fit who we are in Christ. Just as footsteps take us to a destination, so will our words. We want to be known for keeping promises, telling the truth, being faithful to loved ones as well as passers-by…not as someone who "doesn't walk the talk... says one thing; does another… all talk; no action." We can maintain the compass of our hearts on a true course by keeping our word in matters large and small…to God as well as to those long-lost friends and acquaintances.

Conversations at the Kitchen Table

- Do you carefully think through the costs of a commitment before making it?

- Are you keeping even small, tossed-off-at-the-last second promises?

- Are white lies creeping into your conversation, perhaps to spare someone's feelings or keep yourself out of hot water? There are ways to be truthful without heavy camouflage. When you are known for honesty, even if it's a tinge painful, people will trust you to give them the straight, unvarnished truth. Your word will always be good.

- Keep confidences. If a friend has confided personal business and asked you to keep it quiet and someone asks you for details, don't engage in "Don't tell anyone else, but…"

- Try to identify any *"little foxes" (Song of Songs 2:15)* that are raiding your garden and ask God to help you to eliminate them!

- The Bible says the tongue is a small instrument but *"a restless evil, full of deadly poison" (James 3:8)*.

- Read and discuss *James 1:26* and *3:3-12*.

Lavish "Living with Purpose" Lunch

Today's menu is great for entertaining or packing up for your neighborhood block party. Sit back and enjoy the raves!

Pasta Primavera with Sun-Dried Tomato Cream Sauce
Favorite pasta (we like tri-colored half moons)
2 cups broccoli florets
2 cups cauliflower florets
1 cup sliced fresh mushrooms
1 small zucchini, diced
1 (28-ounce) can crushed Roma tomatoes
1 (16-ounce) jar sun-dried tomato Alfredo sauce

Heat water for pasta. Steam broccoli and cauliflower for four minutes. Meanwhile sauté mushrooms and zucchini. In a medium saucepan, heat together crushed tomatoes and sun-dried tomato Alfredo sauce. Drain pasta and place in a serving bowl. Add vegetables and sauce and serve with freshly grated Parmesan cheese.

Cranberry-Nut Tartlets
Pastry
1 stick butter
1 (3-ounce) package cream cheese
1 cup flour

Filling
2-1/2 cups fresh cranberries
1/3 cup water
2 tablespoons orange juice
1 cup sugar
2 tablespoons flour
1 tablespoon butter, cut up
1/3 cup finely-chopped walnuts

Preheat oven to 350 degrees. Make pastry by combining softened butter, cream cheese and flour. Form into walnut size balls and press into bottom and up the sides of mini-muffin pans. Meanwhile, combine cranberries, water and juice in saucepan. Bring to boil, stirring 2-3 minutes until berries "pop." Transfer mixture to a small bowl and stir in sugar, flour, butter and nuts. Spoon the filling into pastry cups and bake for 30 minutes. Cool and sprinkle with powdered sugar.

31

Cultivating Our Fruit Stands

They will know us by our fruit

Any time we plant, we expect a harvest. We watch, patiently waiting for the day when sprouts shoot forth from the rocky soil followed by leaves, buds, blossoms and finally branches weighed down with an abundance of fruit. When Christ has been planted in our hearts, our Heavenly Father also patiently, expectantly watches for the first new shoots of faith and good works that sprout evidence of the hope that's been planted in us.

It's thrilling to watch things grow…to note every change and new development. We grow quickly bored with our possessions precisely because they don't change. They're the same decades later as the day we purchased them and soon cease to hold our interest. A garden and a child, however, never stop growing, changing, and becoming new every morning. They hold our interest and fascinate us in ways that enthrall us as well as vex us. Beautiful as they are, it takes hard work and many long days to help them grow and thrive. But no endeavor is more worthy of our time, attention and investment. Our Heavenly Father feels the same way about His children and the garden He's placed in the hearts of those who have received His Son.

Jesus calls us to bear fruit. He says to us *"I am the true vine, and my Father is the gardener. He cuts off every branch in me that bears no fruit, while every branch that does bear fruit he prunes so that it will be even more fruitful"(John 15:1-2).*

As followers of Christ, what fruit should be found in us? *Galatians 5:22* spells them out: *"The fruit of the Spirit is love, joy, peace, patience, kindness, goodness, faithfulness, gentleness, and self-control."* The Holy Spirit instills these fruit seeds in us when we receive Christ and begins to plow the hard ground of our hearts to enable us to bring those seeds to fruition.

Can we possess these qualities without the help of the Holy Spirit? Sure…a bucket-full perhaps, but not in quantities that will withstand the onslaught of life's trials. The supply in the storehouses we develop will burn out and dry up in the sweltering heat of our daily burdens. With the Holy Spirit working in us, however, we will manifest an abundant harvest of fragrant, sweet-tasting fruit no matter how many gauntlets we run or dragons we have to slay…a supply we can draw upon that's infinite!

Entire books can be written on each fruit, but we'll keep our preview to a snapshot while we indulge in a dish of walnut-apricot torte alongside a cup of fragrant lemon-infused tea. Ready? Let's unwrap and sample our fruit baskets:

Love – the coin of the realm in the heavenly kingdom. Nothing is more highly prized. It's why God created man...why Jesus came to rescue us and bring us home...why the Holy Spirit comes to dwell in our muddy abodes and starts housecleaning! Love is the fruit out of which all the other fruits of the Spirit spring forth. Love is the crown jewel...encircled about by each of the remaining fruits, reflecting another brilliant facet of love's glory. Jesus was asked, "Teacher, which is the greatest commandment?" He replied, *"Love the Lord your God with all your heart and with all your soul and with all your mind. This is the first and greatest commandment. And the second is like it: Love your neighbor as yourself"* (Matthew 22:37-39).

> *"Love covers over a multitude of sins"* (1 Peter 4:8).
> *"These three remain: faith, hope and love. But the greatest of these is love"* (1 Corinthians 13:13).

Joy – Happiness flows out of favorable circumstances and transient emotion, but joy resonates from our spirit and transcends whatever hardships or difficult circumstances we face. Joy renews our strength, enabling us to stand up to life's fiercest battles.

> *"The joy of the Lord is your strength"* (Nehemiah 8:10).
> *"You have made known to me the path of life; you will fill me with joy in your presence, with eternal pleasures at your right hand"* (Psalm 16:11).
> *"...joy unspeakable and full of glory"* (1 Peter 1:8 KJV).

Peace – Peace can be our constant companion no matter what sorrow, heartbreak or calamity threatens. God drapes His cloak of peace around us as we keep Him the center of our focus.

> *"You will keep in perfect peace him whose mind is steadfast, because he trusts in you"* Isaiah 26:3).
> *"Though an army besiege me, my heart will not fear"* (Psalm 27:3).
> *"And the peace of God, which transcends all understanding, will guard your hearts and your minds in Christ Jesus"* (Philippians 4:7).

Patience – Patience is energy held in reserve for exactly the right moment. Patience knows how to wait with confidence for the optimum time and occasion that brings about the desired outcome.

> *"A patient man has great understanding"* (Proverbs 14:29).
> *"But they that wait upon the Lord will renew their strength"* (Isaiah 40:31 KJV).

Kindness – Kindness is the tenderest of emotions, revealing a soft and open heart with genuine affection and concern for another, seeing to their care and welfare. Jesus is the picture of kindness as the Good Shepherd as he loved and tended, indeed sacrificed His life, for those in His sheepfold.

> *"I have drawn you with loving kindness"* (Jeremiah 31:3).

"I am the good shepherd. The good shepherd lays down his life for the sheep"
(John 10:11).

Goodness – Goodness is everything that is pure, wholesome, valuable and highly esteemed in the kingdom of God.

"Finally brothers, whatever is true, whatever is noble, whatever is right, whatever is pure, whatever is lovely, whatever is admirable – if anything is excellent or praiseworthy – think about such things"(Philippians 4:8).

Faithfulness – Faithfulness is a promise of devotion to never leave or abandon a loved one. It's an unwavering commitment and loyalty to another no matter what transpires.

"Your faithfulness continues through all generations" (Psalm 119:90).
"Because of the Lord's great love, we are not consumed, for his compassions never fail. They are new every morning; great is your faithfulness" (Lamentations 3:22-23).
"Whoever comes to me I will never drive away" (John 6:37).

Gentleness – Gentleness is a baby being rocked to sleep…cared for and loved in a setting as soothing and tender as a mother's caress. Gentleness is Jesus tending His sheep.

"Take my yoke upon you, and learn from me, for I am gentle and humble in heart, and you will find rest for your souls" (Matthew 11:29).
"And God will wipe away every tear from their eyes" (Revelations 7:17).

Self-Control – Self-control is a discipline not easily mastered but essential in reining in emotions, desires and passions that, if left unchecked, will send our lives into tailspins.

"He who ignores discipline despises himself, but whoever heeds correction gains understanding" (Proverbs 15:32).
"He that is slow to anger is better than the mighty; and he that ruleth his spirit than he that taketh a city" (Proverbs 16:32 KJV).

Here is a fruit stand worth cultivating! This seed packet is a welcome package from God to all those who receive His Son. Every Christian heart has been plowed and seeded. Nearby is the Bible, an instruction book with all the information on how to till, water, weed, provide light and fertilize to ensure an abundance of fruit. God Himself will prune our vines to produce an even greater crop, *John 15:2.* We need only to guard our hearts to maintain the right environment for our seeds to grow and flourish. *"Still other seed fell on good soil. It came up and yielded a crop, a hundred times more than was sown" (Luke 8:8).*

"No good tree bears bad fruit, nor does a bad tree bear good fruit. Each tree is recognized by its own fruit. People do not pick figs from thornbushes or grapes from briers. The good man brings good things out of the good stored up in his heart, and the evil man brings evil things out of the evil stored up in his heart. For out of the overflow of his heart his mouth speaks"(Luke 6:43-45).
"By their fruit, you will recognize them" (Matthew 7:16).

Conversations at the Kitchen Table

- Do you see evidence of the "fruit of the spirit" growing in your heart and having expression in your everyday life?

- Measure your thoughts, attitudes, speech, reactions, habits and practices against *Galatians 5:22*. Grade yourself from 1-10 with 1 as the lowest and 10 as the highest expression of fruit. If there are a number of low fruit scores, commit to one and challenge yourself to come up higher.

- How do we cultivate them if we find ourselves coming up short? Read *Galatians 5:24.*

- Are there some fruits that you find more difficult to cultivate than others?
  If so, pray for more grace in these areas. God provides everything we need to live a productive, fruitful Christian life, but we make choices that enhance or hinder our growth. Study the following passages in *2 Peter 1:1-8:*

  "His divine power has given us everything we need for life and godliness through our knowledge of him who called us by his own glory and goodness. Through these he has given us his very great and precious promises, so that through them you may participate in the divine nature and escape the corruption in the world caused by evil desires."

  "For this reason, make every effort to add to your faith goodness; and to goodness, knowledge; and to knowledge, self control; and to self control, perseverance; and to perseverance, godliness; and to godliness, brotherly kindness; and to brotherly kindness, love. For if you possess these qualities in increasing measure, they will keep you from being ineffective and unproductive in our knowledge of our Lord Jesus Christ."

Lavish "Farmer's Market" Lunch

Salmon is a must-eat at least several times a week to insure enough omega 3 and 6 oils that do wonders for hair, skin and nails. Be sure it's ocean caught and not farm-raised. Save room for dessert…this Walnut-Apricot torte is a show-stopper!

Salmon Chowder with Corn and Potatoes
1 medium onion, diced
1-1/2 cups sliced fresh mushrooms
1/2 pound potatoes, diced
1 (32-ounce) carton organic vegetable stock
1 package frozen organic corn, thawed
1 cup milk
1 dash pepper
1/2 teaspoon salt
2 tablespoons fresh, chopped parsley
1 (15-ounce) can salmon

In a soup kettle or stock pot, sauté onions and mushrooms in olive oil until tender. Add diced potatoes with organic vegetable stock. Bring to a boil then reduce to a simmer. When potatoes are tender, scoop half of the mixture into a food processor or blender and puree. Spoon puree back into the pot. Puree half of the corn, adding milk to make a smooth mixture. Spoon back into the pot along with the rest of the corn, seasonings and salmon. Serve with buttery, herbed biscuits.

Walnut-Apricot Torte
Cake
1 cup butter
1 cup sugar
3 eggs
1 cup finely-crushed walnuts
1/3 cup flour
1 teaspoon grated lemon zest

Filling and Frosting
2/3 cup apricot preserves
1 (8-ounce) package cream cheese
1 teaspoon vanilla
5-6 drops Stevia (a natural, non-caloric, sweet-tasting alternative to sugar)

Preheat oven to 350 degrees. Cream together butter and sugar with mixer for several minutes until light. Beat in eggs one at a time, beating 1 minute after each addition. Beat in nuts until just incorporated. Fold in lemon zest and flour. Bake in two lightly greased and floured 9-inch cake pans for 25-30 minutes. Spread apricot preserves between cake layers. Combine remaining ingredients and frost top layer with cream cheese frosting.

32

Forgiveness-Part I: When Our Hearts Scream No

Trusting God to bring it about in our hearts

Forgiving those who have wronged us is one of the most difficult Scriptural principles to grasp, much less practice. Forgiveness doesn't seem hard most of the time, as some of the things we forgive people for are the very things we know we've done ourselves… canceling plans at the last minute, a hurtful remark, forgetting an important birthday or anniversary, blowing up over a disagreement.

Then there are the hammer blows we never saw coming. Suddenly forgiveness seems not only impossible but the wrong response to such a wretched act. A child is kidnapped… a husband empties the bank account and runs off with another woman…a family member is killed by a drunk driver. Though years may have passed, just the memory releases a new flood of pain that tears savagely at the heart, ripping open wounds as fresh and stinging as the day it took place.

Forgive these people? We'd rather stab them in the neck. If a million years went by we'd be no closer to forgiving such a despicable act than we are now. Maybe God can forgive these wretches, but we can't…and won't. Yet God says we must. Even when it seems to us that forgiving this unforgivable offense is tortuous and unbearably cruel, God is after what's best for us.

Please listen carefully…God knows we have no capacity, no fortitude for this. He knows our hearts are broken and splashing out a bitter brew of hatred and venom over the treachery that's been visited upon us. He suffers with us and doesn't ask us to pretend it's okay…to feel kindly…to drum up empathy or to try to muster up strength to force our hearts into submission. He knows that's impossible - completely beyond us and out of reach. This is a work only He can accomplish by working it out through us and in us.

His desire is only that we trust Him enough to give Him access to our hearts … to tell Him, "Father I can't…and don't want to…forgive this treachery. Nevertheless because your word is clear that I must forgive, I give you permission to do the work in my heart that only you can do. I'm not capable of forgiveness in my heart, but I'm willing to be made willing." That's all He needs. We leave the outcome to Him…for our healing, for our ability to come to a place of forgiveness as well as for the ultimate fate of our transgressors. Be sure of this: in time they will be broken…either on their knees in deep remorse and repentance before God…or by His wrath. *"It is mine to avenge; I will repay. In due time their foot will slip; their day of disaster is near and their doom rushes upon them"* *(Deuteronomy 32:35).*

Whatever ambush or knife-in-the-heart betrayal we might face, be certain that the Son of God has been there before us. Jesus' response to the agony He suffered is the same one God our Father wants to replicate in us: *"When they hurled their insults at him, he did not retaliate; when he suffered, he made no threats. Instead, he entrusted himself to him who judges justly"* *(1 Peter 2:23).*

> *"Love your enemies, do good to those who hate you, bless those who curse you, pray for those who mistreat you"* *(Luke 6:27, 28).*

Conversations at the Kitchen Table

- Is there someone in your life you need to forgive?

- Can you begin to view the situation through God's eyes?

- Will you take this situation to God and ask for His help in softening your heart toward this person?

- Whatever this person has done to wound you, they have done through fear, ignorance or a heart hardened by sin, and they are in desperate need of the saving grace and forgiveness of Christ…just as we are. Will you begin to pray for this person and ask God to help you to forgive and to take the next step as He directs?

Lavish "Warm our Hearts" Lunch

We came up with two favorite menu items for today's sobering message. The sweet treats are pure bliss…a little bite of heaven as we meditate on forgiveness!

Chicken-Broccoli Stroganoff

1 cup fresh sliced mushrooms
3 tablespoons flour
3 tablespoons butter
2 cups chicken broth
1 cup reduced-fat sour cream
2 cups cooked chicken, cut into bite-size pieces
2 cups steamed broccoli florets
Salt and pepper
Whole wheat noodles

Prepare noodles per package directions. Meanwhile, sauté mushrooms in 2 tablespoons of butter. Add flour and additional tablespoon of butter to make a paste. Add broth and bring to a low boil, stirring until mixture is smooth and thickened. Add sour cream, stirring until blended. Add chicken, broccoli and seasonings. Serve over hot noodles.

Surprise Blind Date Cookies

36 pitted dates
Walnut pieces
1/2 cup butter
3/4 cup brown sugar
1 egg
1/2 cup sour cream
1-1/4 cups sifted all purpose flour
1/2 teaspoon baking powder
1/2 teaspoon baking soda
1/4 teaspoon salt

Preheat oven to 400 degrees. Cut walnuts to size to fit into each date. Cream butter and sugar and beat in the egg. Stir in sour cream. Sift together dry ingredients and stir into creamed mixture. Carefully fold in each of the prepared stuffed dates. Scoop up a tablespoon of batter along with one date; place on a greased cookie sheet, leaving 1-inch between each cookie. Bake 5-7 minutes or until cookies are lightly golden. Cool on rack. Sprinkle with a heavy dusting of powdered sugar (all blind dates should be this sweet!)

33

Forgiveness Part II:
The Metal Jacket of Unforgiveness
Unforgiveness sends our hearts to the deep freeze

Jesus tells a story about the terrible price we pay for a spirit of unforgiveness in *Matthew 18: 23-35*. A king calls a servant to account for a debt of 10,000 talents. The servant could not repay such a huge amount of money and the king was prepared to have him and his family sold into slavery to repay the debt. The servant pleaded for mercy and patience and the king, having compassion upon him, forgave the entire debt.

The freed servant then encountered someone who owed him a very small amount of money. Rather than responding in a similar way to the man's plea for mercy, he had him thrown into jail until he could repay the tiny sum. The king learned of this cold-hearted act and had the servant brought before him. He asked the servant *"Shouldn't you have had mercy on your fellow servant just as I had on you?"* (Matthew 18:33). He then delivered the servant to the jailers to be tormented until he could come up with what he owed.

> *"Forgive us our debts, as we also have forgiven our debtors" (Matthew 6:12).*

> *"And when ye stand praying, forgive, if ye have aught against any: that your Father also which is in heaven may forgive you your trespasses. But if ye do not forgive, neither will your Father which is in heaven forgive your trespasses" (Mark 11:25-26 KJV).*

Why won't our heavenly Father forgive us if we don't forgive others? Closing off our hearts to another in unforgiveness renders us incapable of receiving God's mercy. His shower of forgiveness splashes off the metal jacket encircling our hearts without penetrating that icy, frozen tundra. It's not that God can't forgive us…it's that we've hardened ourselves against it.

Christ died to forgive every sin we've ever committed. Since we have received so gracious a pardon, how can we then withhold the same from those who have wronged us? No matter what we think we can't forgive, Scripture models those who have. The Bible is full of figures that learned to forgive the unforgivable and received God's blessings. Following are just a few of these stories you might be interested in reading:

> Esau forgives Jacob, *Genesis 33:4, 11*
> Joseph forgives his brothers, *Genesis 45: 5-15, 50:19-21*
> David forgives Saul, *1 Samuel: 24:10-12, 26:9, 23*
> Jesus forgives his enemies, *Luke 23:34*

"'Lord, how many times should I forgive my brother, when he sins against me? Up to seven times?' Jesus replied, 'I tell you, not seven times, but seventy-seven times'" (Matthew 18: 21, 22).

Conversations at the Kitchen Table

- Has it been helpful to see that unforgiveness towards anyone hardens our hearts and blocks the mercy of God for our own transgressions?

- If you can identify anyone that you have been unwilling or unable to forgive, are you willing to ask God to help you slip out of the "metal jacket of unforgiveness" and permit Him to do the work in your heart that will free you from bitterness and resentment?

- It's helpful to remember that harboring hatred and rage in our hearts is like ingesting a powerful poison that wreaks havoc and widespread damage in our physical bodies. Thoughts of revenge and getting even? Don't go there. Read *Romans 12:17-21*. Give the situation to God and trust Him to work it out.

- If any of the friends gathered with you are struggling with unforgiveness, stop now and pray that God will soften their hearts and lead them on the path to forgiveness. If you're the one having difficulty, ask your friends to pray for you to release this burden and lay it at the foot of the cross.

Lavish "Olive Branch" Lunch

We pray that you didn't find these forgiveness messages hard to swallow. Today we're headed for the tropics with our Fish Bake on the Bay and Tropical Sunrise Cookies. Let's dream of sand white beaches, warm Caribbean waters and a tropical sun that will surely melt any frost that has settled over our hearts!

Fish Bake on the Bay
2 cups brown rice
1 cup chicken broth
2 teaspoons Old Bay seasoning, divided
1 pound firm fresh white fish (halibut, cod or tilapia)
2 cups sliced mushrooms
1 small onion, chopped
2 garlic cloves, minced
1 red pepper, chopped
1 teaspoon curry powder
1 jar (14-ounce) artichoke hearts, drained and quartered
3-4 tablespoons fresh lemon juice
1/4 cup fresh chopped parsley
1 cup (divided) shredded Bistro blend cheese: Cheddar, Monterey Jack, Tomato and Jalapeno
Salt and pepper to taste

Preheat oven to 350 degrees. Cook rice in chicken broth. Meanwhile, sprinkle fish with one teaspoon Old Bay seasoning and broil or grill 8-10 minutes. Lightly sauté mushrooms, onions, garlic, red peppers and combine with cooked rice, artichoke hearts, remainder of Old Bay, curry powder, parsley and half of the cheese. Spoon mixture into 13x9-inch baking dish, arranging fish over the rice. Sprinkle with remaining cheese and bake for 20 minutes.

Tropical Sunrise Cookies
1 cup sugar
2 1/2 cups flour
1/4 teaspoon salt
1/4 teaspoon baking soda
3/4 cup butter
3 ounces cream cheese
1 egg
1 tablespoon orange zest
2 tablespoons orange juice

Frosting
1-1/2 cups powdered sugar
Several tablespoons orange juice to desired consistency
1/4 cup coconut

Preheat oven to 375 degrees. Mix dry ingredients. Cream together butter and cream cheese. Add sugar and beat until blended. Add egg, zest and juice, mixing well. Stir in flour mixture. Wrap and chill dough for several hours. Drop cookie dough by heaping teaspoons onto greased cookie sheet. Bake for 8-10 minutes. Frost when cooled.

34

Trade in All Those Self Help Books
Only one dispenses divine wisdom

God addresses every need, every dilemma and every situation we will ever face in the pages of Scripture. In our search for enlightenment, however, we're scrambling to buy the next "how to" best seller that promises all the answers on how to get ahead, make more money, find a career, save a marriage, raise kids, motivate employees, be your own boss, start a business, as well as how to juggle all of the above with the latest time management principles. Yet buying just one Bible can save us the time, trouble and expense of any number of these books because we're investing in God's wisdom rather than man's.

When all the self-help books have been read, they sit on the shelf. We've extracted every tip, technique, practice and protocol. We've scoured every page for anything that might give us an edge. Now they're collecting dust because they have nothing new to say, what they did offer was a temporary fix, or didn't hit the mark at all. In a few weeks, we're off to the bookstore looking for the next best-seller that might tell us something we haven't already heard.

God's book, however, continues to speak to us all the days of our lives. The more we return to the pages of His book, the more we gain deeper levels of wisdom, practical advice that sometimes makes no worldly sense but proves itself out in the end. Reading and applying what we read over time brings about a different cadence to our steps, a new perspective and sensitivity in our thoughts, a reordering of our priorities. It can provide a radical shift in the longitude and latitude of the maps that help us navigate the stormy seas of life.

"My son, if you accept my words and store up my commands within you, turning your ear to wisdom and applying your heart to understanding, and if you call out for insight and cry aloud for understanding, and if you look for it as for silver and search for it as for hidden treasure, then you will understand the fear of the Lord and find the knowledge of God. For the Lord gives wisdom, and from his mouth come knowledge and understanding. He holds victory in store for the upright, he is a shield to those whose walk is blameless, for he guards the course of the just and protects the way of his faithful ones. Then you will

understand what is right and just and fair – every good path. For wisdom will enter your heart, and knowledge will be pleasant to your soul. Discretion will protect you, and understanding will guard you" (Proverbs 2:1-11).

There's no self-help book in the world that can dispense divine wisdom. Why go to them when the source of all wisdom, the Lord God Almighty, awaits in the pages of the Bible, willing to reveal and unfold before us His vision, His plan and purpose for our lives? Who better to ask for direction? Where else to seek advice and counsel? What better door to knock upon for help?

"Ask and it will be given to you; seek and you will find; knock and the door will be opened to you. For everyone who asks receives; he who seeks finds; and to him who knocks, the door will be opened" (Matthew 7:7, 8).

Conversations at the Kitchen Table

- Are there a number of self-help books lining your bookcase?

- Is there a Bible on the shelf or hidden in a drawer or closet you'd be willing to dust off?

- Do you see the wisdom in seeking the counsel of the one *"who by his understanding made the heavens…who spread out the earth…who made the great lights…the sun to govern the day…the moon and stars to govern the night…"(Psalm 136:5-9),* rather than mere mortals?

- If you haven't already done so, consider beginning a prayer journal and review it every few months. It will build your faith and confidence to see how many prayers God has answered and help you to develop patience for the requests you still seek.

- What does Scripture say about seeking God for wisdom and guidance? Check out the following Scripture verses:

Psalm 16:5-8
Psalm 18:16-36
Psalm 19:7-14

Lavish "Enlightenment" Lunch

Chicken Manicotti
1 package manicotti
2 pounds chicken breasts, cut up
Extra virgin olive oil
2 cups fresh sliced mushrooms
1 small onion, finely chopped
2 cloves garlic, minced
1 (15-ounce) carton ricotta cheese
1 (15-ounce) carton cottage cheese
2 lightly beaten eggs
1 (8-ounce) package shredded mozzarella
1/4 cup fresh chopped parsley
2 teaspoons Italian seasoning
1 jar favorite pasta sauce
Parmesan cheese

Preheat oven to 350 degrees. Prepare manicotti per package directions. Sauté chicken pieces in olive oil along with mushrooms, onions and garlic until chicken is cooked and vegetables are tender. Set aside. Mix together ricotta cheese, cottage cheese, beaten eggs, mozzarella and seasonings and stir in chicken mixture. Spoon several tablespoons of pasta sauce on the bottom of a 13x9-inch baking pan. Stuff manicotti pieces with chicken-cheese filling and place side-by-side in prepared pan. Spoon pasta sauce over manicotti and sprinkle generously with Parmesan. Bake 35-40 minutes. Serve with mixed green salad and Italian bread.

Fruit Bars
1/2 stick butter
3/4 cup sugar
2 eggs
1 teaspoon vanilla
1 (15-ounce) can crushed pineapple (well drained)
1/2 cup mashed banana
2 cups sifted all-purpose flour
1-1/2 teaspoons baking powder
1 teaspoon salt
1/4 teaspoon nutmeg
1 cup chopped walnuts
1 cup pitted chopped dates

Glaze
Powdered sugar
Lemon juice
Milk

Cream butter and sugar, then add eggs and vanilla and mix well. Drain pineapple and add to creamed mixture along with bananas. Resift flour with baking powder, salt and nutmeg. Add to batter. Mix in nuts and dates. Spread in greased 15x10-inch pan. Bake for 20-25 minutes or until lightly golden. Cool, then spread with lemon glaze. Cut into bars.

35

Running on Empty: The Five Foolish Virgins
The Boy Scout motto applies: Be Prepared

*A*rlene writes…Jesus told His disciples a parable about five wise and five foolish virgins in *Matthew 25:1-13*. All 10 virgins were awaiting the bridegroom and upon his arrival, all would accompany him to the wedding feast. However, only five of the virgins properly prepared themselves to meet him. They had their lamps lit and their oil jars by their side to replenish the lamps should the oil run out. The foolish ones also had lamps, but did not take any additional oil.

The wait lasted long into the night and the virgins all fell asleep. At midnight they were awakened by the news that the bridegroom had indeed arrived and it was time to go meet him. By this time the lamps were going out and the foolish virgins asked the wise virgins to share their oil. They replied there would not be enough for them both and suggested they go purchase some. While they were gone, the bridegroom arrived and the wise virgins went with him to the banquet hall and the door was closed.

Later the foolish virgins arrived and asked to enter the banquet hall. The bridegroom replied, *"I tell you the truth, I don't know you" (Matthew 25:12)*. This cautionary tale ends with instructions to *"Therefore keep watch because you do not know the day or the hour" (Matthew 25:13)*. This story reminds me of the time my dad called my sister and me away from an evening of play in a neighbor's backyard to return to the house pronto. When we arrived, he critiqued our after-dinner chores, pronouncing them "half-baked." We had washed, dried and put away the dishes, but neglected to clear the dinner table of crumbs and sweep the floor. In our haste to meet our friends for play, we left behind a messy kitchen that did not pass muster. "Don't be careless and do a half-baked job," my dad instructed as we set about sweeping the floor and sponging the table.

This is the way it was with the five foolish virgins. They were awaiting the bridegroom who represents Christ, but they were totally unprepared! They thought they had a relationship with the bridegroom, but it was half-baked, as my dad would say. They were going through the motions, but their hearts were at play in someone else's backyard.

The Apostle Paul cautioned the early church not to take their salvation for granted. *"Examine yourselves to see whether you are in the faith; test yourselves"* (2 Corinthians 13:5). Once saved, good works should also be in evidence, displaying the work of the Holy Spirit. *James 2:26 says, "Faith without works is dead."* Let's watch for His coming, be faithful in carrying out our appointed tasks, and live each day as if it's the one we'll meet Jesus. Then we'll be certain to have our lamps lit and a ready supply of oil at our side!

"Be dressed ready for service and keep your lamps burning…" (Luke 12:35).

"…live holy and godly lives as you look forward to the day of God and speed its coming" (2 Peter 3:11, 12).

Conversations at the Kitchen Table

Paul asks us to examine ourselves to see whether we are in the faith. In such a test, we first must be able to identify a specific time in our lives when we asked Christ to be our Lord and Savior. If that's the case, good works and charitable deeds should be in evidence in our lives as the outflow of a changed heart. We need to be careful, however, in thinking that good works by themselves, without having received Christ, will ever measure up to God's standard of perfection.

- Can you pinpoint a time in your life when you asked Christ to be your Lord and Savior?

- Is Christ alone your hope of glory?

- Is there evidence of good works or charitable deeds in your life prompted by the Spirit of God who lives in you?

Hebrews 13:16
James 2:14-17

Lavish "Wise Women's" Lunch

Wise women eat lots of spinach, and we've come up with yet another way to serve it! This Florentine filling raises the humble meatloaf to lofty heights.

Spinach-Mushroom Stuffed Meatloaf
1 (10-ounce) package frozen, chopped spinach (thaw and squeeze dry)
1 cup sliced fresh mushrooms
1 cup chopped onion
2 cloves garlic, minced
1 tablespoon butter
1 cup sour cream
2 eggs
1/2 cup milk
1-1/2 pounds ground beef
3/4 cup breadcrumbs
1 tablespoon Worcestershire sauce
Salt and pepper

Sour Cream Sauce
1 cup sour cream
1-2 heaping tablespoons horseradish

Preheat oven to 350 degrees. Sauté the mushrooms, onions and garlic in butter. Remove from heat and combine with spinach and sour cream. Set aside. Combine remaining ingredients and form three quarters of the mixture into a football shape in a casserole dish. Hollow out the center of the meat and spoon spinach filling into this area and place the rest of the meat mixture over the filling, covering completely. Bake for 50-60 minutes. Let stand 15 minutes before slicing. Serve with sour cream sauce.

Blackberry Torte
1 stick butter
3/4 cup sugar
3 eggs, separated
1 cup ground walnuts
1/3 cup blackberry preserves
1-1/2 teaspoons vanilla
1-1/2 cups sifted cake flour
1-1/4 teaspoons baking powder
Powdered sugar

Preheat oven to 350 degrees. Beat butter in mixing bowl until light. Gradually beat in sugar. Add egg yolks, one at a time, beating well after each addition. Stir in the nuts, blackberry preserves and vanilla. Sift the flour with the baking powder. Beat the egg whites until stiff but not dry and fold both mixtures alternately into the batter.

Pour batter into buttered and floured 9-inch springform pan. Bake 40-45 minutes. Cool, unmold and place on a cake platter. Dust with powdered sugar.

36

When the Wicked Thrive
The joyride is all too brief

Decades ago a Detroit drug kingpin was killed. His funeral was lavish... an over-the-top, money's no object affair, and he went out the way he lived: with an entourage, a column of limos and dressed to the nines. Hundreds of people lined the streets as his hearse passed by to pay homage to this larger-than-life homeboy who had scaled the heights of money, power and fame.

In his brief life, he had amassed a fortune, conquered his known world and was surrounded by a crowd of "wanna-be" pretenders to his throne. It didn't matter that his riches came at the expense of thousands enslaved to the netherworld of drugs, or that his own life was cut short by a rival drug gang. The throngs lining the street to glimpse his motorcade hailed him as a hero, a crown prince.

Trying to live a Christ-like life, meanwhile, can seem pale in comparison when we're up against cramped living quarters, difficult bosses, long hours at work, money woes and overdue bills. Reading about yet another mob boss or drug dealer newly acquitted and free to return to mansions and a bevy of cars in five-stall garages makes it easy to question whether justice really prevails.

In this world, however, everything is not as it seems. When the wicked thrive while the godly suffer hardship and injustice, many make an assumption that crime does indeed pay handsomely and abandon the path of righteousness. This road, however, leads to utter ruin and the enticing trinkets and toys it offers along the way are not worth the ultimate price to be paid. *"Do not fret because of evil men or be envious of the wicked, for the evil man has no future hope, and the lamp of the wicked will be snuffed out" (Proverbs 24: 19, 20).*

A glamorous life fueled by sin is a brief one followed by an eternity of remorse. Christ spells this out for us in *Mark 8:36* when he asks *"What good is it for a man to gain the whole world, yet forfeit his soul?"* He asks the question, and answers it by directing us to seek a different path: *"Enter through the narrow gate. For wide is the gate and broad is the road that leads to destruction, and many enter through it. But small is the gate and narrow the road that leads to life, and only a few find it" (Matthew: 7:13).* The narrow path leaves little room for excess worldly baggage and none at all for ungodly practices and sensual indulgences. It may demand the loss of every "must have" we think is essential to our happiness, but to trade eternal salvation for a short-term ride on an earthly merry-go-round is utter folly.

Choosing the narrow path calls for placing our trust in God for the discipline, patience and wisdom to bring about a satisfying life here as well as an eternity filled with the riches of His glorious Kingdom. *"Blessed is the man who does not walk in the counsel of the wicked or stand in the way of sinners or sit in the seat of mockers. But his delight is in the law of the Lord, and on his law he meditates day and night. He is like a tree planted by streams of water, which yields its fruit in season and whose leaf does not wither. Whatever he does prospers"* *(Psalm 1:1-3).*

"To him who overcomes, I will give the right to eat from the tree of life, which is in the paradise of God" (Revelation 2:7).

Conversations at the Kitchen Table

- Have you ever questioned God's justice when you see or read about wicked people who seem to have it all?

- Does this message help you to see that God's justice will prevail in the end? Read *Hebrews 4:13*.

- Has hardship, loss or injustice ever caused you to doubt whether God truly loves you or cares about your situation? Read *Psalms 121* and *138:7, 8*.

- Whatever trial or crisis you may be bearing, trust God and He will not waste your pain.

Romans 8:17, 18
James 1:2-4
2 Corinthians 4:8-18

Lavish "Cross the Finish Line" Lunch

The finish line is out there far beyond our sight line. We'll reach it with full confidence if we *"...throw off everything that hinders and the sin that so easily entangles, and let us run with perseverance the race that is marked out for us" (Hebrews 12: 1)*. We offer our version of comfort food today. Throw in potatoes and cauliflower for this rich, thick soup and substitute vegetable broth for water that imparts tons of flavor. Nobody will be looking for the missing ham!

Peas and Potato Potash
1 (32-ounce) carton vegetable broth
2 cups water
1 package dried peas
2 carrots, sliced
2 celery stalks, sliced
1 onion, diced
1 large or 2 small potatoes, cubed
1 cup cauliflower florets (optional, but a great way to use up any extra cauliflower)
Salt and pepper to taste

Combine all of the above ingredients in a large soup pot or kettle. Bring to a boil, then cover and lower heat to a simmer. Check in 40 minutes to see if mixture needs additional liquid. Cover and cook additional 20 minutes. Serve with whole-grain rolls.

Cream-filled Banana-Oatmeal Cookies
1 cup softened butter
1 cup sugar
1 egg, beaten
1-1/2 cups flour
1/2 teaspoon baking soda
1 teaspoon cinnamon
1/4 teaspoon nutmeg
1-1/2 cups rolled oats
1 cup mashed ripe bananas (2-3)
1/2 cup chopped nuts

Orange Cream
1 (8-ounce) package cream cheese
1/4 cup honey
2-3 tablespoons orange juice

Cream together butter, sugar and egg. Add flour, baking soda, spices and rolled oats, mixing until blended. Drop rounded teaspoonfuls about 2 inches apart on ungreased baking sheet. Bake 10-12 minutes. When cool, sandwich cookies together with orange cream.

37

The Divine Exchange
We always get the better trade

There'll never be a time where we give to God and don't get something back. And we always get the better end of the deal. God's nature is to give. He gives us life. He gives us His word. He gives us His Son whose shed blood covers our sins. He gives us the Holy Spirit to train us in righteousness. He gives us a fresh start, a clean slate, a new future. He gives us unconditional love. He gives us faith, hope and a crown of glory. He gives us the keys to His kingdom where He's building a mansion that awaits us in glory. He gives us the right to call Him Father.

He gives first: *"While we were still sinners, Christ died for us" (Romans 5:8).*

He does the initiating: *"We love him because he first loved us" (1 John 4:19).*

He then begins a lifetime of taking our meager, paltry offerings in exchange for His riches in glory:

Our offenses for grace: *"…for all have sinned and fall short of the glory of God and are justified freely by his grace through the redemption that came by Christ Jesus"(Romans 3:23, 24).*

Our water into wine: *"Jesus said to the servants, 'Fill the jars with water;' so they filled them to the brim. Then he told them, 'Now draw some out and take it to the master of the banquet.' They did so, and the master of the banquet tasted the water that had been turned into wine. He did not realize where it had come from…he called the bridegroom aside and said 'Everyone brings out the choice wine first and then the cheaper wine after the guests have had too much to drink; but you have saved the best till now' "(John 2:7-10).*

Our seven fish and five loaves into a meal for the multitudes: *"They sat down in groups of hundreds and fifties. Taking the five loaves and the two fish and looking up to heaven, he gave thanks and broke the loaves. Then he gave them to his disciples to set before the people. He also divided the two fish among them all. They all ate and were satisfied" (Mark 6:40-42).*

Our weariness for rest: *"Come to me, all you who are weary and burdened, and I will give you rest" (Matthew 11:28).*

Our corrupt natures for His divine nature: *"He has given us his very great and precious promises, so that through them you may participate in the divine nature and escape the corruption in the world caused by evil desires"(2 Peter 1:4).*

Our thirst for streams of living water: *"'If anyone is thirsty, let him come to me and drink. Whoever believes in me, as the Scripture has said, streams of living water will flow from within him'" (John 7:37).*

Our poverty for His riches: *"And my God will meet all your needs according to His glorious riches in Christ Jesus." (Philippians 4:19)*

Our ashes for beauty: *"...to bestow on them a crown of beauty for ashes..." (Isaiah 61:3).*

Our darkness for light: *"For you were once darkness, but now you are light in the Lord" (Ephesians 5:8).*

Our freedom from captivity: *"He has sent me to proclaim freedom for the prisoners and recovery of sight for the blind" (Luke 4:18, KJV).*

Our sorrow for gladness: *"Gladness and joy will overtake them, and sorrow and sighing will flee away" (Isaiah 51:11).*

Our heavy hearts for a garment of praise: *"...a garment of praise instead of a spirit of despair" (Isaiah 61:3).*

Our wasted years for restoration: *"I will restore to you the years the locusts have eaten" (Joel 2:25, KJV).*

Our impossible with His possible: *"With man this is impossible, but with God all things are possible" (Matthew 19:26).*

When we give Him what little we have, He develops it, enlarges it, embellishes it, expands it, increases it, multiplies it, magnifies it, purifies it, protects it, restores it, repairs it, revives it, resuscitates it, re-energizes it, resurrects it, galvanizes it and glorifies it. In His kingdom, there's no shortage, no last slice of the pie. With Him there's abundant supply, a never-ending storehouse of provision.

He asks us to believe in Him, trust what He says and take Him at His word. Then watch what He will do through us with just the tiniest measure of faith: *"I tell you the truth, if you have faith as small as a mustard seed, you can say to this mountain, 'Move from here to there' and it will move. Nothing will be impossible for you" (Matthew 17:20).*

Conversations at the Kitchen Table

- Do you see evidence of God's abundant storehouse of provision?

- Have you taken Him up on "the great exchange?"

- If not, we encourage you not to let another minute pass before telling Him you want to receive Christ's shed blood for your sins… to trade your ashes for beauty… your sorrow for His gladness… your lack for His riches in glory… your impossible with His possible!

This is our prayer for you. So many things in life are too good to be true…with God, however, it's all good and it's all true! Make the trade!

"Come near to God, and He will come near to you!" (James 4:8).

Lavish "Trading Up" Lunch

By now you must know that we love to find as many ways to feature spinach and chicken in our main entrees and berries for dessert whenever and wherever possible. So of course, for our last lavish lunch with you, we're featuring all of them! Today's dessert is one we imagine being served at a London manor or a baron's estate in the English countryside. Perhaps Emily Dickinson or the Bronte sisters would have dished up this delightful confection for a Sunday dinner. Enjoy!

Chicken and Vegetable Rustica
Spinach and Potato Crust
4 beaten eggs
1 tablespoon milk
Salt and pepper to taste
3 cups frozen hash brown potatoes
2 (10-ounce) packages frozen chopped spinach (thaw and squeeze dry)
1 cup shredded Monterey Jack-cheddar cheese, divided

Filling
2 pounds chicken breasts, cut into bite-size pieces
1 small onion, quartered, halved, then sliced into strips
1 cup any other vegetable you like or have on hand: cut up broccoli, cauliflower, zucchini, peppers
1 cup sliced fresh mushrooms
1-1/2 cups of sour cream

Combine eggs, milk, salt and pepper; add potatoes, spinach and cheese. Press into bottom and partly up sides of a well-greased 13x9-inch casserole dish. Set aside.

Meanwhile, heat 1-2 tablespoons of butter in a skillet and sauté chicken four to five minutes. Add onion, mushrooms and continue cooking until vegetables are tender. Combine chicken and vegetables with sour cream and cheese and spoon over spinach-potato crust. Bake 40-45 minutes or until heated through. Let stand for five minutes before cutting into squares.

Lemon-Raspberry Trifle
Favorite lemon cake recipe
1 (10-ounce) package frozen raspberries (set aside a handful to top trifle)
3 cups plain yogurt, drained
1/4 cup raspberry preserves
5-6 drops Stevia (non-caloric, natural alternative to sugar)
2 cups heavy cream (whipped cream from a canister will not hold up as well)

Make the lemon cake a day ahead of your lavish lunch. Drain yogurt in cheesecloth inside a strainer in a bowl several hours or overnight in fridge. Before guests arrive, make whipped cream by beating two cups of heavy cream, adding several drops of Stevia to sweeten. In a separate mixing bowl, combine drained yogurt, raspberry preserves, several drops of Stevia to sweeten, then stir in frozen raspberries. To assemble trifle, place a handful of cake pieces in bottom of trifle dish or other glass serving bowl. Spoon several heaping tablespoons of raspberry-yogurt cream over cake pieces, then cover with a generous topping of whipped cream. Repeat layers several times finishing with whipped cream and scattering of fresh berries. Cover and chill until ready to present and serve.

Epilogue

W hat a pleasure it has been to have you sitting at the kitchen table with us throughout this journey of faith. We pray that you have been inspired to try some fun dishes, invite over some friends and neighbors and enjoy a lavish lunch while dishing up hope from God's word.

Throughout the writing of this book, we have laughed, cried, hoped, dreamed, planned, cooked, baked, tested, tasted and prayed…. all in preparation for you to be part of this lavish lunch. We continue to keep you in prayer as well as all those who will be guests at your kitchen table.

In this imperfect world fraught with uncertainty, God is more real to us than anything else in life. We continue to marvel at how he has crafted all the days of our lives into His perfect plan…from walking us through every storm we have faced, to renewing our friendship, to guiding us in writing this book. We want to share a praise report with you that we hope will inspire you as much as it has us! After months of treatment, Julie's latest CAT scan shows no trace of the tumor in her nasal passage! Join us in praising our gracious, glorious God *"who forgiveth all thine iniquities and healeth all thy diseases" (Psalm 103:3 KJV).*

He has been a participant at our kitchen tables, and we hope that you'll set a place for Him at yours. No RSVP needed…He's thrilled with the invitation and always delights in being our guest!

Julie and Arlene
March 2006

Food Tips

W̲e are not expert cooks by any stretch of the imagination. Yet we believe that eating well is within everyone's reach. Simple, well-prepared food using the freshest ingredients possible will always taste better, serve us well nutritionally and please even the pickiest of palettes. We've tried to include a variety of interesting, uncomplicated recipes that are a step above the ordinary, using ingredients that won't require trips to a specialty food store. Fast and easy preparation gets us out of the kitchen to maximize time with family and friends.

We use real food rather than substitutes. No margarine, no egg-beaters, no imitation crab or vanilla. We make our own whipped cream and our own soups. Thankfully, we're not soda-drinkers. If you are, we suggest you cut back or eliminate sodas and train your palette to enjoy herbal teas, fresh fruit smoothies and water with a wedge of lemon. Sodas have no nutritional value and contain sugars and additives that tax your body. Try our raspberry-apple refresher – it's pure and delicious! (Page 128)

Read labels. If we can't pronounce or identify the ingredients, we don't buy it. A splash of extra virgin olive oil and rice vinegar makes an excellent salad dressing. You'll save a ton of space in the refrigerator by eliminating a variety of bottled dressings that also contain chemicals your body doesn't need.

Eat your greens…and yellows, reds and blues! Broccoli, kale, spinach, green, red and yellow peppers, tomatoes, cherries, grapes, strawberries, blueberries, watermelon are colorful, delicious and loaded with good nutrients that fuel your body. Try to fit into your life more meals comprised of raw, organically grown, uncooked fruits and vegetables.

Lightly sauté, steam and roast wherever possible. When fresh produce isn't available, frozen fruits and vegetables work just fine. Steer away from processed, packaged food as much as possible. We make an exception for some canned items such as beans, salmon, tuna, artichoke hearts, pumpkin and tomatoes.

What about desserts? We think life is too short not to indulge in an occasional sweet treat. We especially love cookies and bars because they're easy to bake and are sized for a two-bite indulgence to enjoy with a cup of tea. The rest can be given away or frozen for another day or when unexpected company arrives. We've included a variety of desserts here that will make your lavish lunches special or serve as ideas for the next potluck, bake sale or hostess gift.

A few last thoughts…less is more. Massive, oversized platters of food fit for a lumberjack have long been in vogue, and Americans have the waistlines and backsides to show for it! Our lavish lunches are designed to share…or freeze to enjoy another day. Our bodies will adjust to smaller portions, and we'll be healthier and live longer if we make the effort. Just as important, get in some kind of workout at least three days a week. The body was designed to move and be active. If you're not inclined to sports or a gym, walk! Finally, be strong, be healthy, be happy, friends…until we meet again!

Printed in the United States
59007LVS00008B/37-110